THE
HOTHOUSE
BY HAROLD PINTER

★

★

DRAMATISTS
PLAY SERVICE
INC.

TO HENRY WOOLFE

AUTHOR'S NOTE

I wrote *The Hothouse* in the winter of 1958. I put it aside for further deliberation and made no attempt to have it produced at the time. I then went on to write *The Caretaker*. In 1979 I re-read *The Hothouse* and decided it was worth presenting on the stage. I made a few changes during rehearsal, mainly cuts.

CHARACTERS

ROOTE, *in his fifties*

GIBBS, *in his thirties*

LAMB, *in his twenties*

MISS CUTTS, *in her thirties*

LUSH, *in his thirties*

TUBB, *fifty*

LOBB, *fifty*

THE HOTHOUSE was first presented at Hampstead Theatre, London, in April 1980 in a production directed by Harold Pinter. It moved to the Ambassador Theatre, London, in June 1980.

THE HOTHOUSE was first presented in New York City (the Trinity Square Repertory Company production) at the Playhouse Theatre by Arthur Cantor and Dorothy Cullman, in association with Adrian Hall, on May 6, 1982. It was directed by Adrian Hall; the scenery and lighting design were by Eugene Lee; the costumes were designed by William Lane; and the associate producer was Harvey Elliott. The cast, in order of appearance, was as follows:

ROOTE ....*George Martin*
GIBBS .... *Richard Kavanaugh*
LAMB...*Dan Butler*
MISS CUTTS...*Amy Van Nostrand*
LUSH ....*Peter Gerety*
TUBB .... *Howard London*
LOBB .... *David C. Jones*

ACT I
Christmas morning

ACT II
Christmas night

LOCATIONS

ROOTE's *office*
A stairway
A sitting room
A sound-proof room
LOBB's *office in the Ministry*

THE HOTHOUSE

ACT ONE

Roote's office. Morning. Roote is standing at the window, looking out. Gibbs is at the filing cabinet, examining some papers.

ROOTE. Gibbs.

GIBBS. Yes, sir?

ROOTE. Tell me …

GIBBS. Yes, sir?

ROOTE. How's 6457 getting on?

GIBBS. 6457, sir?

ROOTE. Yes.

GIBBS. He's dead, sir.

ROOTE. Dead?

GIBBS. He died on Thursday, sir.

ROOTE. Thursday? What are you talking about? What's today?

GIBBS. Saturday, sir.

ROOTE. Saturday … Well, for goodness sake, I had a talk with him, when was it? *(Opens his desk diary.)* Recently. Only the other day. Yesterday, I think. Just a minute.

GIBBS. I hardly think yesterday, sir.

ROOTE. Why not?

GIBBS. I supervised the burial arrangements myself, sir.

ROOTE. This is ridiculous. What did he die of?

GIBBS. I beg your pardon, sir?

ROOTE. If he's dead, what did he die of?

GIBBS. Heart failure, sir. *(Roote stares at him, sits at the desk and consults the diary.)*

ROOTE. Wait … here we are. Got it. Conversation with 6457 ten o'clock Friday morning. That was yesterday. Well, what do you make of that?

GIBBS. I'm afraid there seems to be a slight discrepancy, sir.

ROOTE. Discrepancy! I'm damn sure there's a discrepancy! You come and tell me that a man has died and I've got it down here that I had a conversation with him yesterday morning. According to you he was in his grave. There does seem to be a slight discrepancy, I agree with you.

GIBBS. I meant ... about the dates, sir.

ROOTE. Dates? What dates?

GIBBS. In your diary, sir. *(He moves to the desk.)* I must point out that you are in fact referring to Friday, the 17th. *(He indicates a date on the page.)* There, sir. Yesterday was Friday the 24th. *(He turns the pages forward and indicates a date.)* Here, sir. You had a conversation with 6457 on the 17th. He died on the 23rd. *(Indicates a date.)* Here.

ROOTE. What! *(He turns the pages back.)* Good Lord, you're right. You're quite right. How extraordinary. I haven't written a single thing down in this diary for a whole week.

GIBBS. You've held no interviews with any of the patients, sir, during the last week.

ROOTE. No, I haven't, have I? Why not?

GIBBS. You decided on the ... 18th sir, that you would cancel all interviews until further notice.

ROOTE. *(Slowly.)* Oh yes. So I did. *(Gibbs moves round the desk.)*

GIBBS. For the sake of accuracy, sir, I'd like, if I may, to point out to you what is apparently another discrepancy.

ROOTE. Another one?

GIBBS. Yes, sir.

ROOTE. You're very keen this morning, aren't you, Gibbs.

GIBBS. I do try to keep my powers of observation well exercised, sir.

ROOTE. Don't stand so close to me. You're right on top of me. What's the matter with you?

GIBBS. I'm so sorry, sir. *(He steps away from the desk.)*

ROOTE. There's plenty of room in here, isn't there? What are you breathing down my neck for?

GIBBS. I do apologise, sir.

ROOTE. Nothing's more irritating.

GIBBS. It was thoughtless of me, sir. *(Pause.)*

ROOTE. Well ... what was this *other* discrepancy, anyway?

GIBBS. *(Flatly.)* It was not 6457, sir, whom you interviewed on the 17th.

ROOTE. Gibbs.

GIBBS. Sir?

ROOTE. One question.

GIBBS. Sir.

ROOTE. Are you taking the piss out of me?

GIBBS. Most decidedly not, sir. *(Slight pause.)*

ROOTE. All right. You have said it was not 6457 I interviewed on the 17th. What evidence have you got to support your contention?

GIBBS. The figures in your diary, sir.

ROOTE. Figures?

GIBBS. One figure, sir. If I may ... *(He bends over the desk.)* ... this one.

ROOTE. Which one?

GIBBS. This one. It's not a seven, sir. It's a nine.

ROOTE. Nine?

GIBBS. Nine, sir. The number is 645 ... 9.

ROOTE. Good God, so it is. Nine. Well, it's not a very clear nine, is it?

GIBBS. It was in fact 6459 whom you interviewed, sir.

ROOTE. Must have been. That's funny. I wonder why I thought it was seven. *(He rises abruptly.)* The whole thing's ridiculous! The system's wrong. *(He walks across the room.)* We shouldn't use these stupid numbers at all. Only confuses things. Why don't we use their names, for God's said? They've got names, haven't they?

GIBBS. It was your predecessor who instituted the use of numbers, sir.

ROOTE. How do you know?

GIBBS. So I understand, sir.

ROOTE. You weren't even here then.

GIBBS. No, sir.

ROOTE. I was.

GIBBS. Quite, sir.

ROOTE. I was standing where you're standing now. I can tell you that. Saying yes sir, no sir and certainly sir. Just as you are now. I didn't bribe anyone to get where I am. I worked my way up. When my predecessor ... retired ... I was invited to take over his position. And have you any idea why you call me sir now?

GIBBS. Yes, sir.

11

ROOTE. Why?

GIBBS. Because you called him sir then, sir.

ROOTE. Right! *(Pause.)* But I sometimes think I've been a bit slow in making changes. Change is the order of things, after all. I mean it's *in* the order of things, it's not *the* order of things, it's *in* the order of things. *(Slight pause.)* Still, I sometimes think I could have instituted a few more changes — if I'd had time. I'm not talking about many changes or drastic changes. That's not necessary. But on this numbers business, for instance. It would make things so much simpler if we called them by their names. Then we'd all know where we were. After all, they're not criminals. They're only people in need of help, which we try to give, in one way or another, to the best of our discretion, to the best of our judgment, to help them regain their confidence, confidence in themselves, confidence in others, confidence in … the world. What? They're all people specially recommended by the Ministry, after all. They're not any Tom, Dick or … or … er … Harry. *(He stops, brooding:)* I often think it must depress them … somewhat … to have a number rapped at them all the time. After some of them have been here a few years they're liable to forget what names their fathers gave them. Or their mothers. *(Pause.)* One of the purposes of this establishment is to instill that confidence in each and every one of them, that confidence which will one day enable them to say "I am … Gubbins," for example. Not easy, not easy, agreed, but it makes it doubly difficult if they're constantly referred to as 5244, doesn't it? We lose sight of their names and they lose sight of their names. I sometimes wonder if it's the right way to go about things. *(He sits at the desk.)*

GIBBS. Would you like me to place further consideration of this matter on the agenda, sir?

ROOTE. *(Sharply.)* Certainly not. We can't.

GIBBS. Can't, sir?

ROOTE. You know damn well we can't. That was one of the rules of procedure laid down in the original constitution. The patients are to be given numbers and called by those numbers. And that's how it's got to remain. You understand?

GIBBS. Perfectly, sir. *(Gibbs goes to the filing cabinet.)*

ROOTE. A death on the premises?

GIBBS. Sir?

ROOTE. A death? You say this man has died?

GIBBS. 6457, sir? Yes, sir.

12

ROOTE. Which one was he?

GIBBS. You had quite a lot to do with him, actually, sir.

ROOTE. He was a man I dealt with personally?

GIBBS. Yes, sir.

ROOTE. Well, which one was he, for God's sake?

GIBBS. You knew him well, sir.

ROOTE. You keep saying that! But I can't remember a damn thing about him. What did he look like? *(Pause.)*

GIBBS. Thinnish.

ROOTE. Fairheaded?

GIBBS. *(Sitting.)* Not darkheaded, sir. *(Pause.)*

ROOTE. Tall?

GIBBS. Certainly not small. *(Pause.)*

ROOTE. Quite a sharp sort of face?

GIBBS. Quite sharp, yes, sir.

ROOTE. Yes. *(Pause.)* Yes, he had a sharp sort of face, didn't he?

GIBBS. I should say it was sharp, sir, yes.

ROOTE. Limped a bit?

GIBBS. Oh, possibly, a trifle, sir.

ROOTE. Yes, he limped. He limped on his left leg.

GIBBS. His left, sir?

ROOTE. Well, one of them. I'm sure of it.

GIBBS. Yes, he had a slight limp, sir.

ROOTE. Yes, of course he had. *(Pause.)* He had a slight limp. Whenever he walked anywhere … he limped. Prematurely grey, he was. Prematurely grey. *(Pause.)* Yes, I remember him very well. *(Pause.)* He's dead, you say?

GIBBS. Yes, sir.

ROOTE. Then why wasn't I told? It's your job to keep me informed of all developments in this building, no matter how slight, no matter how trivial. I demand an answer. Why wasn't I told?

GIBBS. You signed the death certificate, sir. *(Gibbs goes to the filing cabinet.)*

ROOTE. Did he get a decent burial?

GIBBS. Oh, very decent, sir.

ROOTE. I don't see why I wasn't invited. Who said the last words over him?

GIBBS. There were no last words, sir.

ROOTE. *(Appalled.)* No last words? *(Roote rises, walks to the window, looks out.)* Snowing. Isn't it the patients' exercise time?

GIBBS. Not today, sir.

ROOTE. Why not?

GIBBS. It's Christmas day, sir. *(Roote goes back to the desk and sits.)*

ROOTE. All right, that's all for now. Bear everything in mind. *(He examines some papers. Gibbs does not move. Roote looks up.)* What is it? What are you waiting for?

GIBBS. You asked me a question earlier, sir, which I haven't yet had a chance to answer.

ROOTE. Haven't had a chance? What do you mean? That I've been talking too much or something?

GIBBS. Not at all, sir. We simply passed on to another topic.

ROOTE. *(Regarding him.)* Gibbs.

GIBBS. Sir?

ROOTE. *(Confidentially.)* Between ourselves, man to man, you're not by any chance taking the old wee-wee out of me, are you?

GIBBS. Most assuredly not, sir. By no means. I merely feel it incumbent upon me to answer any questions you put to me, or to do my best to do so. You are dependent upon me for certain information and I feel it in the line of duty to supply you with it, especially when it is by specific request.

ROOTE. Stop mouthing! This has been a most exhausting morning. If the morning's like this what's the rest of the day going to be like? There's no system, that's the trouble. Look. The next time I ask you a question answer it and we won't waste so much time fiddling about. Things are getting much too slack around here. *(Pause.)* Well, come on, what was this question?

GIBBS. You asked me, sir —

ROOTE. Wait! *(He leans forward on the desk. Quietly.)* Before you go on, Gibbs, let me say one thing. Be sure that what you say is accurate. You are about to quote a question you say I put to you. I don't know what you're going to say, but immediately you've said it I shall know whether I said it, or whether I didn't. I shall know.

GIBBS. Yes, sir.

ROOTE. I didn't get this job for nothing, I can assure you. I shall know. Have no doubt whatsoever on that point.

GIBBS. No, sir.

ROOTE. Stick to the facts, man, and we won't go far wrong.

GIBBS. Yes, sir. *(Pause.)*

ROOTE. Well, what was this question?

GIBBS. You asked me how 6459 was getting on, sir. *(Pause.)*

ROOTE. *(Expressionless.)* Did I?

GIBBS. To be quite accurate, sir, it was 6457 you inquired after, but, of course, 6457 is dead. We agreed, after examining certain discrepancies, that it was 6459 you were referring to. *(Pause.)*

ROOTE. *(Expressionless.)* Did we? *(The lights fade on the office. They go up on the sitting room. Miss Cutts and Lamb enter the sitting room.)*

LAMB. That was fun, I must say. You know you really play extraordinarily well, Miss Cutts.

CUTTS. Do I?

LAMB. Oh, excellent. I enjoyed it immensely. *(Miss Cutts sits. Lamb goes to the coffee machine.)* Black or white?

CUTTS. Black.

LAMB. *(Chuckling.)* I must say I got the surprise of my life, you know, when you came up to me this morning and asked me if I played table tennis. What I mean is, considering we've never spoken to each other before. *(He gives her a coffee.)* It was really very nice of you. Do you play often?

CUTTS. Not often.

LAMB. Well, it's a damn good piece of luck that our rotas coincide at this time of the morning, isn't it? It'll be something to look forward to, a game of ping-pong. I haven't played for ages. *(Pause. He sits with his coffee.)* Do you like it here?

CUTTS. Oh, I do. It's so rewarding.

LAMB. Your work?

CUTTS. Terribly rewarding.

LAMB. You've been here some time, of course?

CUTTS. Mmnn. Oh yes.

LAMB. What about Mr. Roote? How do you get on with him?

CUTTS. Oh, such a charming person. So genuine.

LAMB. Yes, I'm sure he is. I haven't really … spoken to him yet. Although I expect I will be meeting him, very soon now. *(He stands, walks about.)* I only wish I had a bit more to do. I'm a very energetic sort of chap, you know. Tremendous mental energy. I'm the sort of chap who's always *thinking* — you know what I mean? Then, when I've thought about something, I like to put it into action. I mean, I think a lot about the patients, you see. *(Pause.)* You have quite a bit to do with them, I suppose?

CUTTS. Mmm … *(Lush walks quickly into the sitting room.)*

LUSH. Have you seen Gibbs?

LAMB. Gibbs? *(Lush goes.)* What a curious thing. Did you hear

that, Miss Cutts? That was Lush. He asked if we'd seen Gibbs. *(Miss Cutts is leaning back in her chair.)*
CUTTS. Mmnn?
LAMB. Lush. Popped his head in the door just now. Asked if we'd seen Gibbs.
CUTTS. And have we?
LAMB. I haven't. *(Pause.)* You know, I … I haven't really got used to this place. *(Pause.)* Do you know what I mean? I wouldn't say this to anyone else but you, of course. The fact is, I haven't made much contact with any of the others. Hogg said good morning to me in a very nice way about a week ago when I bumped into him near the gym, but I haven't seen him since. *(With sudden briskness.)* No, you see, what happened was this — the Ministry said to me, I was working in one of their other departments at the time, doing something quite different — well, anyway, they called me up and they said to me — "You've been posted." Well, I'd heard about this place, of course. I was delighted. But … but what exactly is the post, I said. You'll learn that when you get down there, they said, but we think you've got the right qualifications. *(Pause.)* That's what they said. That was over a year ago. *(Pause.)* And I've never learned who the man was I took over from, and I've never found out why he left, either. Anyway I'm pretty sure he wasn't doing the job I'm doing. Or if he was doing the same job he wasn't doing it in exactly the same way. The whole rota's been altered since he left, for a start. He couldn't have been doing my rota, and if he wasn't doing my rota he can hardly be said to have been doing my job. Rotas make all the difference. *(Pause.)* I mean, my job, for instance. I have to see that all the gates are locked outside the building and that all the patients' doors are locked inside the building. It gives me exercise, I'll say that. It takes me two hours and six minutes, approximately, to try every gate and every door, then I can stand still for ten minutes, then off I go again. I have the regulation breaks, of course. Breakfast, lunch, tea and dinner. Still, I feel a bit whacked when my shift's over. I must admit. But as I said it gives me time to think — not when I'm testing the locks, of course — but in between locks — it gives me time to think, and mostly I think about the patients. I get some very good ideas while I think, honestly. As a matter of fact, I hear one receives a little token of esteem, sometimes — I mean after a certain period. I've got a feeling that mine's almost due. *(Pause.)* Perhaps it might even be promotion. *(Pause.)* Quite frankly, I can't

make much more progress with this job I was allocated. There's not enough scope. I wish I could deal with the patients — directly. I've thought out a number of schemes, you know, ideas, for a really constructive, progressive approach to the patients — in fact, I've sent them in to the office. Haven't heard anything yet. I think possibly what's happening is that on the evidence of these schemes I sent in they're considering promotion. Look, I want to ask you, these schemes of mine — you know, the ones I've sent in to the office — do you think that was the right place to send them, or should I have handed them in personally to someone? The point is, who? *(Miss Cutts looks at her watch. She stands.)*

CUTTS. Will you excuse me? I'm afraid I have an appointment. *(She goes to the door. Lamb follows.)*

LAMB. You're the only friend I've got here, to be quite frank. I don't seem to be able to ... reach the others. Don't know why. After all, I share their interests. Wouldn't you say? *(They go out. The lights fade on the sitting room. They go up on the office. Roote and Gibbs are in the same positions.)*

ROOTE. *(Deliberately.)* Well, how is 6459 getting on?

GIBBS. She's given birth to a boy, sir. *(Pause.)*

ROOTE. She ... has ... what?

GIBBS. Given birth, sir.

ROOTE. To ... a what?

GIBBS. A boy, sir. *(Pause.)*

ROOTE. I think you've gone too far, Gibbs.

GIBBS. Not me, sir, I assure you. *(Roote leans across the desk.)*

ROOTE. Given birth?

GIBBS. Yes, sir.

ROOTE. To a child?

GIBBS. Yes, sir.

ROOTE. On these premises?

GIBBS. On the fourth floor, sir. *(Roote rises, leans over the desk to Gibbs, about to speak, unable to speak, turns, leaves the desk, walks heavily across the room.)*

ROOTE. Sex?

GIBBS. Male. *(Roote sinks on to the sofa.)*

ROOTE. This has made my morning. It really has made my morning. *He takes a pair of glasses out of his pocket, puts them on and looks across the room to Gibbs.)* I'm dumbstruck. Quite thunderstruck. Absolutely thunderstruck! This has never happened before. Never! In all the years I've been here, in all the years my predecessor was here. And I'm quite certain never before him. To spend years and years, winter after winter, trying to perfect the working of an institution so fragile in its conception and execution, so fragile the boundary between the achievement of one's aspirations and their collapse, not only one's own aspirations; rather the aspirations of a whole community, a tradition, an ideal; such a delicately wrought concept of participation between him who is to be treated and him who is to treat that it defies analysis; trying to sustain this fine, fine balance, finer than a … finer than a … far, far finer. Year after year, and so refined the operation that the softest breath, the breath of a … feather … can send the whole thing tottering into chaos, into ignominy, to the death and cancellation of all our hopes. Goodness gracious. *(He stands.)* As my predecessor said, on one unforgettable occasion: "Order, gentlemen, for God's sake, order!" I remember the silence, row upon row of electrified faces, he with his golden forelock, his briar burning, upright and commanding, a soldier's stance, looking down from the platform. The gymnasium was packed to suffocation, standing room only. The lucky ones were perched on vaulting horses, hanging without movement from the wallbars. "Order, gentlemen," he said, "for the love of Mike!" As one man we looked out of the window at Mike, and gazed at the statue — covered in snow, it so happened, then as now. Mike! The predecessor of my predecessor, the predecessor of us all, the man who laid the foundation stone, the man who introduced the first patient, the man who, after the incredible hordes of patients, or would-be patients, had followed him through town and country hills and valleys, waited under hedges, lined the bridges and sat six feet deep in the ditch, opened institution after institution up and down the country, rest homes, nursing homes, convalescent homes, sanatoria. He was sanctioned by the Ministry, revered by the populace, subsidised by the State. He had set in motion an activity for humanity, of humanity and by humanity. And the key word was order. *(He turns to Gibbs.)* I, Gibbs, have tried to preserve that order. A vocation, in fact. And you choose Christmas morning to come and tell me this. I tell you quite frankly I smell disaster.

GIBBS. With respect, sir, I can't see that the matter is of such extreme significance.

ROOTE. You can't? Have we ever, to your knowledge, given birth to a child on these premises before?

GIBBS. Not to my knowledge, sir.

ROOTE. Therefore we have no yardstick. As a mathematician you will appreciate that we have nothing to measure this event by so that we can with ease assess its implications.

GIBBS. I am not a mathematician, sir.

ROOTE. Well, you look like one! *(He pockets his glasses, sits at the desk.)* Right! There's work to be done. Find the culprit! Who is he?

GIBBS. That, sir, we have not yet been able to ascertain.

ROOTE. Why not? Have you asked the patient?

GIBBS. Yes, sir.

ROOTE. What did she say?

GIBBS. She was ... noncommittal, sir. She said she couldn't be entirely sure since most of the staff have had relations with her in this last year.

ROOTE. Most of the staff?

GIBBS. According to her statement, sir. *(Roote rubs his mouth.)*

ROOTE. Which one *is* 6459?

GIBBS. She's a woman in her thirties —

ROOTE. That means nothing to me, get on with it, what does she look like? Perhaps I know her.

GIBBS. Oh, there's no doubt that you know her, sir.

ROOTE. What does she look like? *(Pause.)*

GIBBS. Fattish.

ROOTE. Darkheaded?

GIBBS. *(Sitting.)* Not fairheaded, sir. *(Pause.)*

ROOTE. Small?

GIBBS. Certainly not tall. *(Pause.)*

ROOTE. Quite a sensual sort of face?

GIBBS. Quite sensual, yes, sir.

ROOTE. Yes. *(Pause.)* Yes, she's got a sensual sort of face, hasn't she?

GIBBS. I should say it was sensual, sir, yes.

ROOTE. Wobbles when she walks?

GIBBS. Oh, possibly a trifle, sir.

ROOTE. Yes, she wobbles. She wobbles in her left buttock.

GIBBS. Her left, sir?

ROOTE. Well, one of them. I'm sure of it.

GIBBS. Yes, she has a slight wobble, sir.

ROOTE. Yes, of course she has. *(Pause.)* She's got a slight wobble. Whenever she walks anywhere ... she wobbles. Likes eating toffees, too ... when she can get any.

GIBBS. Quite true, sir. *(Pause.)*

ROOTE. No — I don't think I know her. *(Pause.)* And you say a number of the staff have had relations with this woman, do you?

GIBBS. Apparently, sir.

ROOTE. *(Standing.)* Well, one of them's slipped up, hasn't he? One of them's not been using his head! His know-how! Common or garden horsesense! I don't mind the men dipping their wicks on occasion. It can't be avoided. It's got to go somewhere. Besides that, it's in the interests of science. If a member of the staff decides that for the good of a female patient some degree of copulation is necessary then two birds are killed with one stone! It does no harm to either party. At least, that's how I've found it in my experience. *(With emphasis.)* But we all know the rule! Never ride barebacked. Always take precautions. Otherwise complications set in. Never ride bare-backed and always send in a report. After all, the reactions of the patient have to be tabulated, compared with others, filed, stamped and if possible verified! It stands to reason. *(Grimly.)* Well, I can tell you something, Gibbs, one thing is blatantly clear to me. *Someone* hasn't been sending in his report!

GIBBS. Quite sir.

ROOTE. *Who? (Gibbs sits on the sofa and puts his hand to his mouth.)*

GIBBS. I think I know the man.

ROOTE. Who?

GIBBS. *(Thoughtfully.)* Yes, it's suddenly come to me. How absurd I didn't realise it before.

ROOTE. Who, for God's sake?

GIBBS. I'd prefer to have the matter verified, sir, before I ... bring him before you.

ROOTE. All right. But find him. The good name of this establishment depends on it. *(Roote sits at the desk. Gibbs goes to the door.)*

GIBBS. What shall I do about the baby, sir?

ROOTE. Get rid of it.

GIBBS. The mother would have to go with it, sir.

ROOTE. Why?

GIBBS. Can't live without the mother.

ROOTE. Why not?

GIBBS. The mother feeds it.

ROOTE. I know that! Do you think I'm an idiot? My mother fed me, didn't she?

GIBBS. Mine fed me.

ROOTE. But mine fed me! *(Pause.)* I remember. *(Pause.)* Isn't there a wet nurse in the house? If there's a wet nurse in the house the baby can go with the wet nurse and the mother can stay here.

GIBBS. There's no wet nurse among the staff, sir.

ROOTE. I should hope not. I'm thinking about the understaff, the kitchen staff, the cleaning staff. Find out if there's a wet nurse among the understaff and get the thing in motion.

GIBBS. Don't you think the mother might miss the baby, sir?

ROOTE. I won't miss it. Will you miss it?

GIBBS. No, sir. I won't miss it.

ROOTE. Then why should the mother miss it? *(They stare at each other. There is a knock on the door.)* Who is it?

CUTTS. Me.

ROOTE. Gibbs, find that father. Come in! *(Enter Miss Cutts.)*

CUTTS. *(To Gibbs.)* Hullo.

GIBBS. I'll keep you in touch with developments, sir.

ROOTE. That's very thoughtful of you. *(Gibbs goes out. Miss Cutts sits on the sofa. Roote rises, goes to the sofa and sits next to her.)* I'm exhausted.

CUTTS. You know, I think that man's frightened of me.

ROOTE. Rubbish.

CUTTS. He never speaks to me. He never says a single word to me. And not only that, he never … he never looks at me. I can only think I must frighten him in some way.

ROOTE. What do you mean, never speaks to you? He's obliged to speak to you. You're working together, aren't you?

CUTTS. Oh yes, he talks shop to me. We discuss patients, naturally. We were discussing one of the patients … only yesterday. But he never speaks to me socially.

ROOTE. Which patient?

CUTTS. Or do you think he's taken with me? Do you think that he just finds me too attractive to look at?

ROOTE. Which patient were you discussing?

CUTTS. But I can't say I like him. He's so cold. Oh, I like men to be cold — but not as cold as that. Oh, no, he's much too cold. You know, I think I'll ask him. I think I'll ask him whether he's taken with me or whether I frighten him. I mean, one might as well know.

ROOTE. Do you know what I've just heard? One of the patients has just had a baby.

CUTTS. A baby? But how?

ROOTE. As large as life. And under my auspices. It's nothing short of criminal.

CUTTS. But how did she manage it?

ROOTE. She had an accomplice.

CUTTS. No? Who?

ROOTE. That's what we've got to find out.

CUTTS. But which patient? Who is she?

ROOTE. I don't know her. *(Miss Cutts leans back.)*

CUTTS. *(Dreamily.)* I bet she feels very feminine now.

ROOTE. *(Vacantly, staring into space.)* She's always been feminine.

CUTTS. Do you think I'm feminine enough, darling? Or do you think I should be more feminine? *(Roote is still abstracted.)* Darling. You don't think I'm too masculine, do you? I mean, you don't think I could go even further? Do you?

ROOTE. *(Absently, muttering.)* Yes, yes why not?

CUTTS. You *do* think I should be more feminine?

ROOTE. What?

CUTTS. But you always say I'm feminine enough!

ROOTE. You are feminine enough.

CUTTS. Then if I'm feminine enough why do you want me to be more feminine?

ROOTE. I don't, I don't.

CUTTS. But you just said you did!

ROOTE. I don't, I don't!

CUTTS. *(At a great pace.)* Because it would be awful if you really thought that I was letting you down in the most important aspect of the relationship between any man and any woman —

ROOTE. You're quite feminine enough!! *(Pause.)*

CUTTS. You really mean it?

ROOTE. Yes. *(He runs his hand through his hair.)* I've had the most wearing morning. On top of everything else one of the patients has died.

CUTTS. Died?

ROOTE. Dead.

CUTTS. Oh my poor sweet, and I've been nasty to you. *(She kisses him.)* Let me massage you. Come into the bedroom. Let me do your neck.

ROOTE. Yes. Do my neck. *(They go into the bedroom. The lights go down on the office. They go up on the sitting room. Gibbs enters. He sits at the low table, takes out a pack of cards and begins to play patience, very deliberately. Lush appears at the head of the stairway and descends. Suddenly a long sigh is heard, amplified. Lush stops. Gibbs, about to place a card, stops. A long keen is heard, amplified. Lush looks up. Gibbs, card in hand, looks up. A laugh is heard, amplified, dying away. Silence. Lush descends the steps, enters the room.)*

LUSH. Hullo, Charlie. *(He closes the door and comes to the table. Gibbs, after a glance at him, places another card. Lush inspects the state of the game. Gibbs scatters the cards.)* How's tricks, Charlie? *(Pause.)* What have you been doing with yourself? *(Pause.)* Mmnn? *(Pause.)* Having a nice Christmas?

GIBBS. What do you want?

LUSH. What do you think of the weather? *(Gibbs collects the cards and puts them into a card case.)*

GIBBS. You want something. What is it?

LUSH. I don't want anything, Gibbs. I've got something to report, that's all.

GIBBS. What is it?

LUSH. Don't get tense, Gibbs. After all, we're all buddies, aren't we? We're all in the game together.

GIBBS. You want to report something. What is it?

LUSH. Actually I want to ask you something first.

GIBBS. What?

LUSH. How's 6459 getting on? *(Pause.)*

GIBBS. You want to report something. What is it?

LUSH. I hear she's given birth.

GIBBS. It's none of your business.

LUSH. Oh, we're all concerned, you know. We're all concerned.

GIBBS. Listen, Lush. I'm not prepared to have any kind of conversation with you whatsoever. If you've got something to report report it and don't make a fool of yourself.

LUSH. Are you the father, Gibbs? *(Gibbs sits back and folds his arms.)* Or the old man. Is the old man the father? *(Lush sits.)* Who's going to carry the can? Miss Cutts? Do you think she's the father? We're all terribly excited, you know. Can't think what to call it. The kid's got to have a name, after all. What do you think yourself? I think something that'll remind him of this establishment when he grows up, don't you? His birth place. Of course, it depends on the father's name, doesn't it? I mean, the father might like the boy to be named after him. You know, if the father's name was John then the boy would be named John too. Do you see what I mean? The same name as the father.

GIBBS. You know, Lush, I don't know how you've lasted here. You're incompetent, you're unwholesome and you're offensive. You're the most totally bloody useless bugger I've ever come across.

LUSH. I can see you're in one of your moods today, Gibbs, so I suppose I'd better report to you what I came to report to you.

GIBBS. What is it?

LUSH. The mother of 6457 came to see me today.

GIBBS. The mother of 6457?

LUSH. Yes, you know. The one who died. He died last Thursday. From heart failure.

GIBBS. His mother?

LUSH. Yes.

GIBBS. How did she get in?

LUSH. That's what baffled me. It did. It quite baffled me. How on earth did she get in? I wondered. How did she do it? Why wasn't she stopped? Why did no-one demand her credentials? It baffled me. Then — in a flash! — the answer came. She'd been hiding all night in the shrubbery, waiting for Tubb to leave his cubby-hole and take a leak, which eventually he did, and then she just darted in, like a shot off a shovel. Simple. We really tend to overlook the simple cunning of the simple. Would you like her description?

GIBBS. No. What did she want?

LUSH. She wanted to know how her son was getting on. She said that when her son came here she was told he needed peace and expert attention and that she would be hearing from us in due course, and that in fact it was now a year since she had seen him and she wanted to know how he was getting on.

GIBBS. What did you say?

LUSH. I said — A year? You haven't seen him for a year? But that's ridiculous. Didn't you come down for Mother's Day, or Thanksgiving Day, or for the annual summer picnic for patients, staff, relatives and friends? Weren't you invited to the Halloween Feast, the May Dance, the October Revival, the Old Boys and Girls supper and social? Dancing on the lawn, cold buffets on the flat roof, midnight croquet, barbecued boar by the lake? None of this? I never knew about it, she said. What! I said. The autumn art exhibition, the monthly concert of orchestral music in the band-room, the half-yearly debate on a selected topic, held traditionally in the men's changing room? The pageant? The unveiling? The Festival of One-Act Plays, judged by Miss Daisy Cutts, L.R.M.B.,

A.C.A., our dramatic instructor? You came down, I said, for none of these activities and ceremonies through which we from time immemorial engage and channel our patients' energies? Oh dear, she said, I was never told. Obviously a clerical error, I said, I shall have it looked into. But, I said, it is a shame that you haven't seen him, since he is now departed from us.

GIBBS. What!

LUSH. He was moved some time ago, I said, to a convalescent home. But I thought this was a convalescent home, said 6457's mother. *(He laughs.)* Silly woman. A convalescent home? I countered, no, no, no, not at all, not at all, whatever gave you that idea? This is a rest home. Oh, said 6457's mother. I see. Well, wasn't he getting enough rest here that they had to send him to a convalescent home? Ah, Mrs. 6457, I said, it's not quite so simple as that. It's not *quite* so *simple* as *that*. In a rest home, you see, you do not merely rest. Nor, in a convalescent home, do you merely convalesce. No, no, in both institutions, you see, you are obliged to work and play and join in daily communal activity to the greatest possible extent. Otherwise the concepts of rest and convalescence are rendered meaningless. Don't for a moment either imagine that the terms rest and convalescence are synonymous. No, no, no, no. They represent, you see, stages. Sometimes one must rest first and then convalesce. Sometimes the reverse. Either course, of course, is only decided after the best interests of the patient have been taken into account. So, I continued, you can rest assured that if your son was moved from here to another place it was in his best interests, and only after the most extensive research into his case, the wealth and weight of all the expert opinion in this establishment, where some of the leading brains in this country are concentrated; after a world of time, care, gathering and accumulating of mass upon mass upon mass of relevant evidence, document, affidavit, tape recordings, played both backwards and forwards, deep into the depth of the night; hours of time, attention to the most minute detail, unstinting labour, unflagging effort, scrupulous attachment to the matter in hand and meticulous examination of all aspects of the question had determined the surest and most beneficial course your son's case might take. The conclusion, after this supreme example of applied dedication, was to send your son to a convalescent home, where we are sure he will be content. *(Pause.)* I also pointed out that we had carte blanche from the Ministry. She left much moved by my recital. *(Pause.)*

GIBBS. Thank you for your report, Mr. Lush.

LUSH. No congratulations? *(Gibbs consults his watch and goes to the internal telephone.)*

GIBBS. Will you excuse me?

LUSH. I'll excuse you for the time being, Gibbs. *(He goes out.)*

GIBBS. *(Into the phone.)* 22, please. *(Pause.)* Sir? Gibbs here. I'd like to speak with Miss Cutts, if I may, with reference to that matter we were discussing earlier. Thank you. *(Pause.)* Miss Cutts? I believe you know a man called Lamb. He's on the staff. Yes. I would be obliged if you would collect him and bring him to number one interviewing room. When I join you, perhaps you would be so kind as to go to 1A control room. I shall be glad of your participation. Thank you. *(He replaces the receiver, and leaves the room. The lights fade on the sitting room. The lights go up on the Left stage area, including the stairway. Miss Cutts followed by Lamb appears at the foot of the stairway. They ascend. Miss Cutts is wearing a white coat.)*

LAMB. But what do you think it's all about? I mean, he wanted to see me particularly, did he?

CUTTS. Oh yes. Particularly.

LAMB. *(Stopping.)* But he didn't say why?

CUTTS. No.

LAMB. You know, I don't know why, but as soon as you said "Mr. Gibbs wants to see you," I felt an extraordinary *uplift*. Isn't it amazing? Really, I felt uplifted. I still do, I must say ... *(They go out of sight. The lights come up on the sound-proof room. Miss Cutts and Lamb enter the sound-proof room.)* It's very curious, I know, but I really feel it's ... significant. I mean, why should I suddenly feel uplifted ... You know, I can't help thinking, I know it's very silly of me, but I can't help thinking this is something to do with my promotion. Do you think he's read my schemes? I mean, why else would he send for me when I was on duty? *(Gibbs enters the room from another door. He wears a white coat.)*

CUTTS. Mr. Gibbs, have you met Mr. Lamb?

GIBBS. How do you do?

LAMB. How do you do?

CUTTS. Would you excuse me a minute, please? *(She leaves the room by the other door.)*

GIBBS. Would you take a seat, Mr. Lamb?

LAMB. This one?

GIBBS. Yes, this one. *(Lamb sits.)* I'm delighted to meet you.

LAMB. Thank you. I must say I've always enjoyed my work here tremendously ... I mean, you really get the feeling here that something ... *important* is going on, something really valuable, and to be associated with it in any way can't be seen in any other light than as a privilege.

GIBBS. That's a very heartening attitude.

LAMB. Oh, I really mean it, quite sincerely.

GIBBS. Good. I've heard a great deal about you, you know.

LAMB. Really?

GIBBS. Yes, there's quite a lot I'd like to talk to you about, when we have the time. But in the meanwhile I wonder ... if you'd give me a helping hand?

LAMB. I'd be quite delighted!

GIBBS. That's the spirit! *(With no undue emphasis.)* Miss Cutts, could you come down, please?

LAMB. What did you say?

GIBBS. I beg your pardon?

LAMB. Did you speak to Miss Cutts just now?

GIBBS. Yes, I asked her to come down.

LAMB. But where from?

GIBBS. From room 1A.

LAMB. But did she hear you?

GIBBS. Oh yes.

LAMB. How?

GIBBS. *(Pointing.)* That mike. It's just been switched on.

LAMB. *(Laughing.)* Oh, I see. *(Pause.)* Curious kind of room, isn't it?

GIBBS. It's a sound-proof room. *(Enter Miss Cutts.)* Ah, Miss Cutts. Now, Lamb, what I'd like is for you to help us with some little tests. Will you do that?

LAMB. Tests? I'd be delighted. That's what I hoped I'd be doing when I first came down here.

GIBBS. Really? Good.

LAMB. What kind of tests are they?

GIBBS. Experiments.

LAMB. Oh, I see.

GIBBS. Well, we have a very willing subject, Miss Cutts.

CUTTS. We do.

GIBBS. Oh by the way, Lamb, Merry Christmas.

LAMB. Thanks. Merry Christmas to you. And to you, Miss Cutts.

CUTTS. Thank you. And to you. *(To Gibbs.)* And to you too.

GIBBS. And to you. *(Briskly.)* Now — perhaps you would fit the electrodes to Mr. Lamb's wrists.

LAMB. Electrodes?

GIBBS. Yes.

CUTTS. Could I have your hand, Mr. Lamb? *(Miss Cutts brings an electrode from her pocket and attaches it to Lamb's wrist.)* Now the other one. *(She attaches a second electrode.)*

LAMB. What are they … exactly?

GIBBS. They're electric. You don't feel anything, of course. Best thing to do is forget about them.

CUTTS. Now I'm going to plug in. *(She bends at the wall, where through a hole, three leads protrude. She picks up two and returns to Lamb.)*

GIBBS. Now she's going to plug in. You see the little socket on each of those electrodes? They're for the plug. *(He watches Miss Cutts plug in.)* That's right. First plug in A, then plug in B. Right. Now you're plugged in.

LAMB. Oh, you've … got to be plugged in, have you?

GIBBS. *(With a chuckle.)* Oh yes, got to be plugged in. The leads go right through the wall and up to the control room, you see. We're plugged in the other end.

LAMB. You?

GIBBS. *(Laughing.)* No, no, not me. You. Into the receiving set.

LAMB. Oh, I see. What are these … what are these electrodes for, exactly?

GIBBS. They measure electrical potential on the skin.

LAMB. Oh.

GIBBS. Engendered by neural activity, of course.

LAMB. Oh, of course.

GIBBS. Electrical impulses, in a word. You can imagine how important they are and yet how little we know about them. Right. Now the earphones. *(Miss Cutts stoops, picks up the earphones, attaches them to Lamb's head.)*

LAMB. Earphones?

GIBBS. Yes, same principle. Plugged in at the socket on your head, plugged in at the other end in our control room. *(Cheeringly.)* Don't worry, they're nice long leads, all of them. Plenty of leeway. No danger of strangulation.

LAMB. *(Laughing.)* Oh yes. Good.

GIBBS. By the way, your predecessor used to give us a helping hand occasionally, too, you know. Before you came, of course.

LAMB. My predecessor?

CUTTS. Could you just keep still a second, Mr. Lamb, while I plug in the earphones? *(Lamb is still. She plugs.)* Thank you.

GIBBS. Comfortable?

LAMB. Yes, thank you. My predecessor, did you say?

GIBBS. Yes, the chap you took over from.

LAMB. Oh! Did he really? Oh, good. I've often wondered what he ... did, exactly. Oh good, I'm ... glad I'm following in a tradition. *(They all chuckle.)* Have you any idea where he is now?

GIBBS. No, I don't think I do know where he is now. Do you know where he is, Miss Cutts?

CUTTS. No, I'm afraid I don't.

GIBBS. No, I'm afraid we don't really know. He's not here, anyway. That's certain. Now what I want you to do is to sit perfectly still. Relax completely. Don't think about a thing. That's right. Now you see that light up there. Ignore it. It might go on and off at regular or irregular intervals. Take no notice. Sit perfectly still. Quite comfortable?

LAMB. Yes, thanks.

GIBBS. Jolly good. Don't go to sleep, will you? We're awfully grateful to you, old chap, for helping us.

LAMB. It's a pleasure. *(Gibbs places his hand briefly on Lamb's shoulder. Miss Cutts and Gibbs go out. Lamb sits. Silence. He shifts, concentrates. The light, which is red, flicks on and off. Silence. Suddenly Lamb jolts rigid, his hands go to his earphones, he is propelled from the chair, falls to his knees, twisting from side to side, still clutching his earphones, emitting high-pitched cries. He suddenly stops still. The red light is still flickering. He looks up. He sits in the chair, emits a short chuckle. The red light stops. The voice of Miss Cutts is heard.)*

CUTTS. Would you say you were an excitable person? *(Lamb looks up.)*

LAMB. Not ... not unduly, no. *(The voice of Gibbs is heard.)*

GIBBS. Would you say you were a moody person?

LAMB. Moody? No, I wouldn't say I was moody — well, sometimes occasionally I —

CUTTS. Do you ever get fits of depression?

LAMB. Well, I wouldn't call them depression, exactly —

GIBBS. Would you say you were a sociable person?

LAMB. Well, that's not a very easy question to answer, really. I try, I certainly try to be sociable, I mean I think it should be the aim of anyone interested in human nature to try to mix, to better his understanding of it. I —

CUTTS. Do you find yourself unaccountable happy one moment and unaccountably unhappy the next?

LAMB. It's strange you should say that because —

GIBBS. Do you often do things which you regret in the morning?

LAMB. Regret? Things I regret? Well, it depends what you mean by often, really. I mean, when you say often —

CUTTS. Are you often puzzled by women?

LAMB. Women?

GIBBS. Men.

LAMB. Men? Well, I was just going to answer the question about women —

GIBBS. Do you often feel puzzled?

LAMB. Puzzled?

GIBBS. By women.

LAMB. Women?

CUTTS. Men.

LAMB. Uh — now just a minute, I ... do you want separate answers or a joint answer?

CUTTS. After your day's work, do you ever feel tired, edgy?

GIBBS. Fretty?

CUTTS. Irritable?

GIBBS. At a loose end?

CUTTS. Morose?

GIBBS. Frustrated?

CUTTS. Morbid?

GIBBS. Unable to concentrate?

CUTTS. Unable to sleep?

GIBBS. Unable to eat?

CUTTS. Unable to remain seated?

GIBBS. Unable to stand upright?

CUTTS. Lustful?

GIBBS. Indolent?

CUTTS. On heat?

GIBBS. Randy?

CUTTS. Full of desire?

GIBBS. Full of energy?

CUTTS. Full of dread?

GIBBS. Drained?

CUTTS. Of energy?

GIBBS. Of dread?

CUTTS. Of desire? *(Pause.)*

LAMB. Well, it's difficult to say, really — *(Lamb jolts rigid, his hands go to his earphones, he is propelled from the chair, falls to his knees, twisting from side to side, still clutching his earphones, emitting high-pitched cries. The red light flicks on and off. He suddenly stops still. The red light is still flickering. He looks up. He sits in the chair, emits a short chuckle. The red light stops.)*

CUTTS. Are you virgo intacta?

LAMB. What?

CUTTS. Are you virgo intacta?

LAMB. Oh, I say, that's rather embarrassing. I mean, in front of a lady —

CUTTS. Are you virgo intacta?

LAMB. Yes, I am, actually. I'll make no secret of it.

CUTTS. Have you always been virgo intacta?

LAMB. Oh yes, always. Always.

CUTTS. From the word go?

LAMB. Go? Oh yes. From the word go.

GIBBS. What is the law of the Wolf Cub Pack?

LAMB. The cub gives in to the Old Wolf, the cub does not give in to himself.

GIBBS. When you were a boy scout were you most proficient at somersault, knots, leap frog, skipping, balancing, cleanliness, recitation or ball games?

LAMB. Well, actually, I never became a boy scout proper. I was a wolf cub, of course, but I never became a boy scout. I don't know why, actually. I've forgotten ... to be frank. But I was a cub.

CUTTS. Do women frighten you?

GIBBS. Their clothes?

CUTTS. Their shoes?

GIBBS. Their voices?

CUTTS. Their laughter?

GIBBS. Their stares?

CUTTS. Their way of walking?

GIBBS. Their way of sitting?

CUTTS. Their way of smiling?

GIBBS. Their way of talking?

CUTTS. Their mouths?

GIBBS. Their hands?

CUTTS. Their legs?

GIBBS. Their teeth?

CUTTS. Their shins?

GIBBS. Their cheeks?

CUTTS. Their ears?

GIBBS. Their calves?

CUTTS. Their arms?

GIBBS. Their toes?

CUTTS. Their eyes?

GIBBS. Their knees?

CUTTS. Their thighs? *(Pause.)*

LAMB. Well, it depends what you mean by frighten —

GIBBS. Do you ever wake up in the middle of the night?

LAMB. Sometimes, yes, for a glass of water.

GIBBS. Do you ever feel you would like to join a group of people in which group common assumptions are shared and common principles observed?

LAMB. Well, I am a member of such a group, here, in this establishment.

GIBBS. Which establishment?

LAMB. This one.

GIBBS. Which establishment?

LAMB. This one.

GIBBS. You are a member of this establishment?

LAMB. Of course. *(Silence. Looking up.)* Mmnn? Any more questions? I'm quite ready for another question. I'm quite ready. I'm rather enjoying this, you know. Oh, by the way, what was that extraordinary sound? It gave me quite a start, I must admit. Are you all right up there? You haven't finished your questions, have you? I'm ready whenever you are. *(Silence. Lamb sits. The red light begins to flick on and off. Lamb looks up, stares at it. We hear the loud click of a switch from the control room. The microphone in the room has been switched off. The red light gradually grows in strength, until it consumes the room. Lamb sits still.)*

Curtain.

ACT TWO

Roote's office. Night. Roote is at his desk, examining some papers. Lush is at the window, looking out.

ROOTE. *(Without looking up.)* What are you looking at, Lush?
LUSH. The yard, sir.
ROOTE. Anyone about?
LUSH. Not a soul.
ROOTE. What's the weather like?
LUSH. The snow has turned to slush.
ROOTE. Ah. *(Pause.)* Has the wind got up?
LUSH. No. No wind at all. *(Roote turns a page. Muttering.)* No wind, eh? *(He examines the page, then slams it onto the desk.)* I can't read a word of this! It's indecipherable. What's the matter with this man Hogg? Why can't he type his reports out like everyone else? I can't read his writing. It's unreadable.
LUSH. His typewriter's out of action, sir.
ROOTE. What's the matter with it?
LUSH. It seems to have got stuck, sir.
ROOTE. Stuck?
LUSH. It just won't move at all.
ROOTE. Well, there must be an obstacle somewhere. Or something.
LUSH. It looked like rust to me.
ROOTE. Rust? What are you talking about? It's a brand new typewriter. It's a Ministry typewriter. We had a whole cartload sent down from the Ministry — when was it? — a couple of months ago. Brand new. I've still got the invoice somewhere. Rust. Never heard such rubbish. Anyway, I can't sit here all night trying to work this out. *(He puts the papers in a drawer, goes to the drinks cabinet, takes out a bottle of whisky and pours himself a drink.)* I've had enough this week. I never leave this desk, do you know that? Sun up to sundown. Day in day out. It's the price you have to pay for being in command, for being responsible for the whole shoot. As I am. The whole damn shoot. *(He drinks. Lush walks to the cabinet, collects a glass and pours himself a drink.)*

33

LUSH. You do leave this desk quite often, though, don't you sir?

ROOTE. What?

LUSH. I say, in point of fact, you do leave this desk quite often, don't you?

ROOTE. When?

LUSH. When you go and visit the patients, for instance.

ROOTE. That's purely in the line of duty. It's not relaxation. I meant relaxation. I wasn't talking about the line of duty.

LUSH. Oh.

ROOTE. Anyway, I've given up visiting the patients. It's not worth it. A waste of energy.

LUSH. What an extraordinary thing to say, Mr. Roote.

ROOTE. Don't Mr. Roote me.

LUSH. But I never expected to hear you say a thing like that, Mr. Roote.

ROOTE. I said don't Mr. Roote me!

LUSH. But I always understood that you looked upon visits to the patients from the head of this establishment as one of the most important features in the running of this establishment ... Mr. Roote.

ROOTE. Listen! I give you leeway. But don't think I give you that much leeway.

LUSH. No, sir.

ROOTE. Don't think I can't squash you on a plate as easy as look at you.

LUSH. Yes, sir.

ROOTE. As easy as look at you, Lush.

LUSH. Quite, sir.

ROOTE. So don't give me any more lip, you understand me? Otherwise you're liable to find yourself in trouble.

LUSH. You know I harbour no illusions about my position, Colonel.

ROOTE. Don't call me Colonel!

LUSH. But you were a Colonel once, weren't you, Colonel?

ROOTE. I was. And a bloody good one too.

LUSH. If I may say so, you still possess considerable military bearing.

ROOTE. Really?

LUSH. Oh yes.

ROOTE. Well, it's not surprising.

LUSH. And the ability to be always one thought ahead of the next man.

ROOTE. It's a military characteristic.

LUSH. Really?

ROOTE. Oh yes. Of course, some of them aren't very bright, I must admit.

LUSH. Who?

ROOTE. Military men.

LUSH. Really? I'm sorry to hear that.

ROOTE. Yes, some of them tend to let the side down. They've got no foresight, that's what it is. They can't think clearly. They've got no vision. Vision's very important.

LUSH. You must have been quite a unique kind of man, sir, in your regiment.

ROOTE. Yes, well I ... what do you mean?

LUSH. The age of the specialist is dead.

ROOTE. What?

LUSH. The age of the specialist is dead.

ROOTE. Oh. Dead. Yes.

LUSH. That's why I say you must have been quite a unique kind of man, sir, in your regiment, being such an all-round man.

ROOTE. Yes, yes, there's something in that. *(He perches on the desk.)*

LUSH. I mean, not only are you a scientist, but you have literary ability, musical ability, knowledge of most schools of philosophy, philology, photography, anthropology, cosmology, theology, phytology, phytonomy, phytotomy —

ROOTE. Oh, no, no, not phytotomy.

LUSH. Not phytotomy?

ROOTE. I was always meaning to get round to phytotomy, of course, but ... well, I've had so many other things to think about.

LUSH. Naturally.

ROOTE. But anyway, once you know something about phytonomy you're halfway there.

LUSH. Halfway where, sir?

ROOTE. To phytotomy! *(Pause.)* Give us a drink. *(Lush fills the glasses.)*

LUSH. Why have you given up visiting the patients?

ROOTE. I've given up, that's all.

LUSH. But I thought you were getting results?

ROOTE. *(Staring at him.)* Cheers.

LUSH. Weren't you getting results?

ROOTE. *(Staring at him.)* Drink your whisky.

LUSH. But surely you achieved results with one patient very recently. What was the number? 6459, I think. *(Roote throws his whisky in Lush's face. Lush wipes his face.)* Let me fill you up. *(He takes Roote's glass, pours, brings the glass to Roote, gives it to him.)* Yes, quite a substantial result, I should have thought. *(Roote throws his whisky in Lush's face. Lush wipes his face. Lush takes Roote's glass, pours, brings the glass to Roote, gives it to him.)* But perhaps I'm thinking of 6457. *(Lush grabs Roote's glass and holds it above his head, with his own. Slowly he lowers his own.)* Cheers. *(He drinks, and then gives Roote his glass.)*

ROOTE. *(Taking the glass, in a low voice.)* You're neglecting to call me sir, Lush. You're supposed to call me sir when you address me. *(Pause. Roote suddenly takes off his jacket, hangs it on the back of his chair and sits.)* God, the heat of this place. It's damn hot, isn't it? It's like a crematorium in here. Why is it suddenly so hot?

LUSH. The snow has turned to slush, sir.

ROOTE. Has it?

LUSH. Very dangerous.

ROOTE. It's a heatwave, that's what it is. *(A knock on the door.)* Who is it? *(Enter Gibbs.)* Oh no, what is it? Business at this hour? You sit down to have a quiet drink and what happens?

GIBBS. I have something to report, sir.

ROOTE. What? *(Gibbs looks at Lush.)* Oh, never mind about him! What is it?

GIBBS. I don't approve of divulging official secrets to all and sundry, sir.

ROOTE. I know you don't approve! I don't approve! Nobody approves! But you've no alternative, have you?

GIBBS. Mr. Lush could leave the room, sir.

ROOTE. Good God, what an impertinence! The man's my guest, do you understand that? Which is more than you bloodywell are! I've never heard of such a thing in all my life. He barges in here and tells me to chuck my own guest out of the room. Who do you think you are? *(Pause. To Lush.)* He gets on my wick sometimes — doesn't he you?

GIBBS. I ... apologise, sir, if I have been presumptuous.

ROOTE. Well, what's your business?

GIBBS. The father has been found.

ROOTE. No?

GIBBS. Found.

ROOTE. *(Rising.)* Found? So soon? In so short a space of time? Jiminy Cricket, that's quick work, Gibbs! *(He stands, shakes hands with Gibbs.)* Absolutely first class! *(He moves to Lush.)* What do you think of that, eh, for a bit of quick work?

LUSH. Remarkable.

ROOTE. You see the way I train my staff? Alacrity! First and foremost, alacrity! Get on with it, don't muck about, don't dither, pick your man and pin him to the wall. Let your nose do your thinking for you and you won't go far wrong. That's what we try to do here, cultivate the habit of split second decisions. Right? Right, Gibbs?

GIBBS. Quite, sir.

ROOTE. Right, Lush?

LUSH. Quite, sir.

ROOTE. And it never fails. I'm pleased with you, Gibbs. Who is he?

GIBBS. A man called Lamb, sir.

ROOTE. Never heard of him. *(Roote sits, pours a drink and drinks.)*

LUSH. Lamb? Surely not Lorna Lamb? Lorna Lamb in the dispensary department?

ROOTE. A man, not a woman, you bloody fool!

LUSH. Oh, I'm so sorry, I didn't quite … What exactly has this person done? *(Pause.)*

ROOTE. Tell him what this person has done, Mr. Gibbs.

GIBBS. A child has been born to one of the patients. It was considered a matter of the first importance to locate the father. This has now been done.

ROOTE. Lamb? Who the hell's Lamb? Do I know him?

GIBBS. I think it doubtful that you've ever met him, sir.

ROOTE. I don't even know what he looks like. A rapist on my own staff and I don't know what he looks like!

LUSH. Was it rape?

ROOTE. Of course it was rape. You don't think that sort of thing happens by consent, do you?

GIBBS. He's not a very important member of your staff, sir.

ROOTE. Well, if he's not important how did he get into the patient's room? You know as well as I do that only a very select handful of the personnel are allowed in the patients' rooms. How did he get in?

GIBBS. He tests the locks, sir, of all the rooms in the building. Either this particular lock was … not locked, or he forced it.

ROOTE. It's unbelievable, isn't it, Lush, the things that go on?

LUSH. It almost is, sir.

ROOTE. The sabotage that goes on, under your very nose. Open the window. I'm suffocating. *(Lush opens the window.)* Is that radiator hot? *(Lush bends to the radiator and touches it.)*

LUSH. Scalding, sir.

ROOTE. That's why I'm so hot.

LUSH. The night is warm, Mr. Roote. The snow has turned to slush.

ROOTE. That's about the fifth time you've said the snow has turned to slush!

GIBBS. It's quite true, sir. I noticed it myself.

ROOTE. I don't care whether it's true or not. I don't like to have a thing repeated and repeated and repeated! Anyone would think I was slow on the uptake. The snow has turned to slush. I heard it. I understand it. That's enough. *(He pours a drink, drinks.)* You think I'm past my job, do you? You think I'm a bit slow? Don't you believe it. I'm as quick as a python.

LUSH. An adder.

ROOTE. What?

LUSH. An adder.

ROOTE. What do you mean, an adder?

GIBBS. Do you think I deserve a little tipple of whisky, sir?

ROOTE. Good God, Gibbs is being jocular. Did you hear that, Lush? He's just made a pleasantry. Didn't you, son? Oh, that's better. I can feel a draught. See if you can turn that radiator off. If we can't turn it off here we'll have to get hold of Tubb and tell him to turn it off at the mains. *(Lush bends to the radiator.)* Well?

LUSH. It won't budge. It's stiff.

ROOTE. It'll have to be turned off at the mains.

LUSH. It's a very cold building, sir, it's perishing on the upper floors.

ROOTE. I tell you it's too bloody hot and the damned heating's got to go off! Who's the boss here, for Christ's sake, you or me?

LUSH. Not me.

ROOTE. I do ten times as much work as the whole lot of you put together. I deserve a bit of comfort, a bit of consideration. The heating will have to be turned off! Every single pipe of it. That's what causes the laxity, the skiving, the inefficiency in this place. It's overheated! Always has been. *(To Gibbs.)* What's the matter with you, standing there like a tit in a trance? Tip the bottle, for the love of Mike. Deserved or undeserved. *(Gibbs pours himself a glass of whisky.)* What do you mean, you deserve it, anyway? You deserve nothing.

GIBBS. I meant for locating the father, sir.

ROOTE. You deserve nothing. Either of you. You've got a job to do. Do it. You won't get any tulips from me. Come on, fill it up, we'll drink a toast. Got yours, Lush?

LUSH. Just a minute. *(Lush pours a glass of whisky.)*

ROOTE. *(Solemnly.)* I'd like to drink a toast.

LUSH. To whom, sir?

ROOTE. I'd like to drink a toast, gentlemen, to our glorious dead.

LUSH. Which ones are they, sir?

ROOTE. The chaps who died for us in the field of action.

LUSH. Oh yes.

ROOTE. The men who gave their lives so that we might live. Who sacrificed themselves so that we might continue. Who helped keep the world clean for the generations to come. The men who died in our name. Let us drink to them. After all, it's Christmas. Couldn't be more appropriate.

LUSH. My glass is ready, sir.

ROOTE. Is yours ready, Gibbs?

GIBBS. It is.

ROOTE. Gentlemen, I give you a toast. To our glorious dead. *(Rising.)*

GIBBS and LUSH. To our glorious dead. *(They drink.)*

ROOTE. A rapist on my own staff and I don't know what he looks like. It's ridiculous. What sort of man is he?

GIBBS. Lamb, sir? Nondescript.

ROOTE. Tall?

GIBBS. No, sir. Small.

LUSH. Tall.

GIBBS. Small. *(Pause.)*

ROOTE. Do you know him, Lush?

LUSH. I've seen him.

ROOTE. Is he fat?

GIBBS. Thin, sir.

LUSH. Fat.

GIBBS. Thin. *(Pause.)*

ROOTE. Brown eyes?

GIBBS. Blue, sir.

LUSH. Brown.

GIBBS. Blue. *(Pause.)*

ROOTE. Curly hair? *(Gibbs and Lush eye each other.)*

LUSH. Straight, sir.

GIBBS. Curly.

LUSH. Straight. *(Pause.)*

ROOTE. What colour teeth?

GIBBS. Lemon, sir.

LUSH. Nigger.

GIBBS. Lemon.

LUSH. Nigger. *(Pause.)*

ROOTE. Any special peculiarities?

GIBBS. None.

LUSH. One.

GIBBS. None. *(Pause.)*

ROOTE. These descriptions don't tally. Next time bring me a photograph. Or you've got a cine-camera. You could devote a half hour film to the man. A documentary — for educational purposes. It's still stifling in here. We'll have to get hold of Tubb. It's uncommonly warm in here for this time of the year, isn't it?

LUSH. It's warm out too. The snow has turned to slush. *(Roote turns, expostulating.)*

GIBBS. Shall I call Tubb on the intercom, sir?

LUSH. I tried the intercom before. It sounded a bit clogged up.

ROOTE. Clogged up? What's the matter with this place? Every-thing's clogged up, bunged up, stuffed up, buggered up. The whole thing's running down hill. I don't like the look of it. Let's see. *(He switches on the intercom on his desk and sits. A voice is heard.)*

VOICE. Number 84. A duck. Who's got ticket number 84? A duck ready for the oven. No-one? Unclaimed, Fred. Next one coming up. Ticket number 21. Number 21. Ten Portuguese cigars. Ten beautiful Portuguese cigars. No-one? Unclaimed, Fred. Number 38. Two tickets to the circus. Two tickets to the circus. Unclaimed, Fred. Number 44. A lovely crockery, cutlery, china and cookery set. Number 44. Unclaimed, Fred. *(Roote switches off.)*

ROOTE. Yes, it does sound a bit clogged up, I must admit. *(He fills the glasses.)* What's it all about?

LUSH. It's the Christmas raffle, held by the understaff in the understaff canteen.

ROOTE. Raffle? Did we get any tickets?

GIBBS. I was approached, sir, but on behalf of the staff declined to purchase any.

ROOTE. Did you? Well, there's a bloody big amount of unclaimed stuff down there, isn't there?

LUSH. Must be a whole pile of it.

ROOTE. Well, who gets it?

LUSH. I expect there'll be another raffle at Easter, sir.

ROOTE. What about that duck? You can't keep a duck until Easter! It's … it's just not sensible! There's not much I don't know about poultry. Lush, make an immediate inquiry as to what's to become of that duck. *(He sits.)*

LUSH. Yes, sir. What about the two tickets to the circus?

ROOTE. Christmas, eh? And I haven't received one present. Not one gift, of any kind. It's most upsetting.

LUSH. Actually, I've seen the duck, sir.

ROOTE. You have? What's it like?

LUSH. It's a dead duck, sir.

ROOTE. Dead?

LUSH. Quite dead, sir.

ROOTE. Good God, I didn't know it was dead.

LUSH. Yes, as dead as patient 6457. If not deader. *(Silence.)*

GIBBS. Is this Ministry whisky, sir? It's quite excellent.

ROOTE. *(To Lush.)* What do you know about 6457?

GIBBS. I wouldn't advise any further discussion of that matter, sir.

ROOTE. What do you know about 6457?

LUSH. I know that he's dead.

ROOTE. What do you know about it?

GIBBS. It is inadvisable to discuss the matter any further, sir.

ROOTE. *(To Lush.)* You're damned clever, aren't you?

LUSH. As a matter of fact, I met a relation of 6457's today.

ROOTE. You what?

GIBBS. Lush. The matter is closed.

ROOTE. What relation?

LUSH. His mother.

ROOTE. How do you know she was his mother?

LUSH. She said so.

ROOTE. She was a liar!

LUSH. No, she wasn't.

ROOTE. How do you know?

LUSH. She looked like a mother.

ROOTE. How do you know what mothers look like?

LUSH. I had one myself.

ROOTE. Do you think I didn't?

LUSH. *(Pointing at Gibbs.)* He didn't.

GIBBS. Oh yes, I did, damn you!

ROOTE. I was fed, Mister Cleverboots, at my mother's breast.

GIBBS. So was I.

LUSH. Me too. *(Sudden silence.)*

ROOTE. WELL? AND WHAT ABOUT IT? *(Roote sinks back in his seat. He looks at his glass, picks it up and swallows the glassful. He chokes, stands, writhes about in a fit of coughing. Gibbs and Lush go to his aid.)*

GIBBS. *(Taking his left arm.)* Come and sit in the armchair, sir.

LUSH. *(Taking his right arm.)* Come and sit on the sofa, sir. *(A short tug-of-war commences, Roote still coughing. Roote shakes them off. He stands, shaking and panting. Lush goes to the desk, picks up a glass of whisky, takes it to Roote.)* Here, drink this, sir. *(Roote viciously knocks the glass out of his hand. He stands, glaring at them, then goes back to his desk, sits. Lush picks up the glass and places it on Roote's desk. Lush fills his glass.)*

ROOTE. 6457's mother, eh? How did she get in? Wasn't the porter on duty at the gate?

LUSH. Don't you want to know what she wanted?

ROOTE. I want to know why the porter wasn't on duty at the gate!

GIBBS. He's in charge of the raffle, sir, in the understaff canteen.

ROOTE. Tubb? That was Tubb just now, on the intercom?

LUSH. Oh, very much Tubb, sir.

ROOTE. Holding a raffle when he should have been on duty at the gate? Honestly, things are going from bad to worse. *(Pouring.)* Down the hatch. *(He raises his glass.)*

GIBBS. Happy Christmas, sir.

ROOTE. Happy Christmas to you, Gibbs.

LUSH. Happy Christmas, sir.

ROOTE. Thank you. Happy Christmas to you, Lush. A happy Christmas to you both.

GIBBS and LUSH. *(Raising their glasses.)* And to you, sir.

ROOTE. Thanks. And the best of luck for the new year.

GIBBS and LUSH. The best of luck for the new year to you, sir. *(A knock at the door.)*

ROOTE. Who's that?

TUBB. Tubb, sir.

ROOTE. Come in. *(Enter Tubb, carrying a small box.)* Tubb! I thought you were on the intercom.

TUBB. Merry Christmas to you, Colonel.

ROOTE. Thank you, Tubb. And to you.

TUBB. How did you enjoy your Christmas dinner, sir?

ROOTE. Disappointing.

TUBB. Oh, I'm sorry to hear that, Colonel.

ROOTE. Too much gravy.

LUSH. Really? Mine was bone dry.

ROOTE. What?

LUSH. Honestly. Bone dry.

ROOTE. Well, mine was swimming in gravy.

LUSH. That's funny, isn't it, Gibbs? His was swimming in gravy and mine was bone dry.

TUBB. I'm surprised to hear yours was wet, Colonel.

ROOTE. Well, it was. Very wet. *(He looks at the box.)* What have you got there, Tubb?

TUBB. It's a Christmas present for you, Colonel.

ROOTE. A present?

TUBB. Just a little token of the understaff's regard, Colonel. Just a little something for Christmas.

ROOTE. Not a duck, by any chance?

TUBB. A duck, Colonel?

ROOTE. I just wondered whether it might have been a duck.

TUBB. Oh no, we haven't got any duck, sir.

ROOTE. No duck?

TUBB. No, sir.

ROOTE. What about number 84 then? Eh? Unclaimed. Ready for the oven. What? That was a duck wasn't it? And what's more it was unclaimed.

TUBB. Oh, that duck. Oh, that was claimed.

ROOTE. *(Startled.)* Claimed? Who by?

TUBB. Well, it wasn't exactly claimed, sir. But we found out who owned the ticket, so we're keeping it for him till he turns up, it's only fair.

ROOTE. Who is it?

TUBB. A man called Lamb, sir. *(Silence.)* But anyway, what I've got here, Colonel, is a little token of regard from the understaff and the compliments of the season from all of us in the understaff, wishing you all the very best of luck in the year to come.

ROOTE. Thanks very much, Tubb. What is it?

TUBB. It's a Christmas cake, Colonel, cooked by the cook.

ROOTE. A cake? For me?

LUSH. That's very nice, isn't it, Gibbs?

ROOTE. A cake? For me?

TUBB. For you, sir.

ROOTE. How kind. How very kind. I'm most touched. Most touched. More than touched. Deeply moved. It's a long time, a very long time, since I had a Christmas cake. A long long time. *(Pause.)* This ... was from the cook?

TUBB. From the cook, sir, from me, sir, from the kitchen staff, sir, from the portering staff, sir, from the cleaning staff, sir, from the very whole of the understaff, sir, from the very all of us ... to you, sir.

ROOTE. How very kind. How very very kind. I'm deeply moved. Deeply moved. More than moved ...

LUSH. What an awfully nice gesture.

TUBB. The understaff, Colonel, and I'm sure the patients, would be even more deeply moved if you were to give them a Christmas address, sir.

ROOTE. An address?

TUBB. They would be most touched, sir. They're all clustered up now in the canteen and I've fitted up the loudspeaker system with an extension to all the corridors leading onto the patients' rooms as well.

LUSH. What a splendid idea.

ROOTE. An address? Your people would appreciate an address, would they?

TUBB. Oh, they would, sir. I know they would. Just a little word for Christmas.

LUSH. What an exciting innovation.

ROOTE. And the patients ... they haven't expressed any desire ... themselves ... have they?

TUBB. Well, not exactly expressed one, sir, as far as I know, but I've fitted up the loudspeaker system to their rooms and I'm sure they'd be deeply moved. *(Pause.)*

ROOTE. What do you think, Gibbs? *(Pause.)* Gibbs!

GIBBS. I beg pardon, sir?

ROOTE. I said what do you think?

GIBBS. I ... I think it's an excellent idea, sir.

ROOTE. Lush?

LUSH. I think it would be deeply moving, sir. *(Pause.)*

ROOTE. *(Briskly.)* Where's the mike?

TUBB. In the cake, sir.

ROOTE. In the cake!

TUBB. I just shoved it in with the cake, sir.

ROOTE. Well, it's got no business to be anywhere near the cake! What's the matter with you? *(Muttering.)* What a place to put a mike!

TUBB. *(Extracting mike.)* Here we are, Colonel.

ROOTE. Well, plug it in, let's get on with it. *(Tubb plugs in by the wall. Roote sits, clears his throat.)*

TUBB. *(With mike.)* On here on the blotting paper all right, sir?

ROOTE. Move out of it.

TUBB. Switch this switch when you're ready, Colonel.

ROOTE. *(Slowly.)* Yes.

TUBB. They're all ready. They're all clustered up in the understaff canteen. *(Pause.)*

ROOTE. What are you looking at, Gibbs?

GIBBS. Nothing in particular, sir.

ROOTE. You were looking at me! Do you call that nothing in particular? *(Pause.)* I can't do it now. I'll do it later on. Later on. You can't make a speech like that without some thought. Tell them not to be disappointed. Tell them they'll hear my Christmas address later on. Later on. *(The lights go down on the office. They go up on the sitting room. Miss Cutts comes in. She sits, takes a table tennis ball from her pocket, tosses it up and catches it. Gibbs descends the stairs. Suddenly a long sigh is heard, amplified. Gibbs stops. Miss Cutts, about to toss the ball, stops. A long keen is heard, amplified. Gibbs looks up. Miss Cutts looks up. A laugh is heard, amplified, dying away. Silence. Miss Cutts puts the ball to her mouth. Gibbs is still a moment, then turns and enters the sitting room. Miss Cutts throws the ball at him. It falls at his feet.)*

CUTTS. Catch! *(Gibbs looks down at the ball and stamps on it.)*

GIBBS. Don't do that. *(He takes out a packet of pills and swallows one.)*

CUTTS. What's the matter, Charlie?

GIBBS. Headache. *(He sits, closes his eyes. Miss Cutts goes to him.)*

CUTTS. Have you got a headache, darling? Come to room 1A. *(She kisses him.)* I'll make it better for you. Are you coming?

GIBBS. I've got to go back.

CUTTS. What! Why?

GIBBS. To hear his Christmas address.

CUTTS. Another one? Oh, God, I thought he'd forgotten all about it.

GIBBS. He hadn't forgotten.

CUTTS. Every year. Sometimes I could scream.

GIBBS. I can't stand screaming.

CUTTS. Charlie, what is it? Don't I please you any more? Tell me. Be honest. Am I no longer the pleasure I was? Be frank with me. Am I failing you?

GIBBS. Stop it. I'm not in the mood.

CUTTS. Let me massage your neck. *(She touches his neck.)*

GIBBS. *(Throwing her off.)* You and your necks! You love to get your hands round someone's neck!

CUTTS. So do you.

GIBBS. I'm not in the habit of touching people's necks.

CUTTS. It was such fun working with you this morning. *(She sits.)* You're so clever. I think you're the cleverest man I've ever had anything to do with. We don't work together nearly enough. It's such fun in room 1A. I think that's my favourite room in the whole place. It's such an intimate room. You can ask the questions and be so intimate. I love your questions. They're so intimate themselves. That's what makes it so exciting. The intimacy becomes unbearable. You keep waiting for the questions to stop, to pass from one intimacy into another, beautifully, and just when you know you can't ask another one, that they must stop, that you must stop, that it must stop — they stop! — and we're alone, and we can start, we can continue, in room 1A, because you know, you always know, your sense of timing is perfect, you know when the questions must stop, *those* questions, and you must start asking me questions, other questions, and I must start asking you questions, and it's question time, question time, question time, forever, and forever and forever.

GIBBS. *(Standing.)* I tell you I'm not in the mood.

CUTTS. Come to 1A, Charlie. *(Gibbs stands, looking at the door.)*

GIBBS. Did you hear anything, just now?

CUTTS. What?

GIBBS. Something. Sounds. Sounds. Just now. Just before.

CUTTS. Nothing. Not a thing. Nothing. *(She looks at him.)* What was it?

GIBBS. I don't know.

CUTTS. *(A nervous chuckle.)* Don't tell me something's going to happen?

GIBBS. Something's *happening*. But I don't know what. I can't … define it.

CUTTS. How absurd.

GIBBS. It is absurd. Something's happening. I feel it, I know it, and I can't define it. It's … it's ridiculous.

CUTTS. I know what's going to happen.

GIBBS. That old fool in there, he sees nothing, getting drunk with that … bitch.

CUTTS. I know what's going to happen. You're going to kill him.

GIBBS. What?

CUTTS. Aren't you? You promised. You promised you would. Didn't you? Do it now. Now. Before he makes his Christmas speech.

GIBBS. Oh, stow it, for God's sake!

CUTTS. But you said you would!

GIBBS. Did I?

CUTTS. You said you'd stab him and pretend it was someone else.

GIBBS. Really? Who?

CUTTS. Lush.

GIBBS. Lush? Lush could never be taken for a murderer. He's scum but he's not a murderer.

CUTTS. No, but you are. *(Gibbs stares at her.)*

GIBBS. *(Quietly.)* What did you say? *(Pause.)* What did you call me?

CUTTS. Nothing.

GIBBS. You called me a murderer.

CUTTS. No, I didn't call you anything —

GIBBS. *(Ice.)* How dare you call me a murderer?

CUTTS. But I didn't!

GIBBS. Who do you know that I've murdered?

CUTTS. No-one!

GIBBS. Then how dare you call me a murderer?

CUTTS. You're not a murderer!

GIBBS. *(Hissing.)* I'm not a murderer, he's a murderer, Roote is a murderer! *(Pause.)* You dare to call me a murderer?

CUTTS. *(Moaning.)* No, Charlie.

GIBBS. You know what that is, don't you? Slander. Defamation of character. *(Pause.)* And on top of that, you try to incite me to kill my chief, Mr. Roote. The man in charge. You, his own mistress. Just to satisfy your own personal whim. *(Pause.)*

CUTTS. Charlie …

GIBBS. Shut up! *(Miss Cutts falls out of her chair onto the floor.)*

CUTTS. *(Whispering.)* Oh, I wish I was in room 1A. I shall never get to room 1A again. I know I won't. Ever. *(Blackout. A drone is heard. The drone stops. Lights go up on the office. Roote and Lush are still drinking. Roote is at the desk, Lush is seated, drooping. Roote rises and perches on the front of the desk.)*

ROOTE. Women! I've known them all. Did I ever tell you about the woman in the blue dress? She was a spy. A spy in a blue dress. I met her in Casablanca. Believe it or believe it not that woman was an agent for a foreign power. She was tattooed on her belly with a pelican. Yes. Her belly was covered with a pelican. She could make that pelican waddle across the room to you. On all fours, sideways, feet first, arse-upwards, any way you like. Her control was superhuman. Only a woman could possess it. Under her blue dress she wore a shimmy. And under that shimmy she wore a pelican. *(Pause.)* My cake! We haven't cut the cake! My God, and it's nearly midnight. *(He unwraps the cake, holds it.)* A beauty. *(Going to his desk drawer.)* Wait a minute. Where are we? Just the thing in here. *(Takes a bayonet from the drawer.)* Now. Right down the middle. *(He cuts the cake.)* I remember the day my walls used to be hung with Christmas cards, I used to walk knee deep in presents, all my aunties and uncles popping in for a drink, a log fire in the grate, bells on the Christmas tree, garlands, flowers, floral decoration, music, flowers ... floral decoration ... laughter ... *(Abruptly.)* I didn't notice a card from you, did I? Didn't expect it either. Because you've no sense of decorum, it sticks out a mile. No heart. It's not so much the language, it's the attitude of mind that's nasty, unwholesome, putrid.

LUSH. The snow has turned to slush.

ROOTE. The temperature must have dropped. *(Thrusting a piece of cake at him.)* Well, here you are, have a piece of this cake. *(Lush stares at it.)* Go on. Eat it! *(They both munch. Lush spits his out. Roote grabs him by the neck.)* What are you doing? That's my cake!

LUSH. I can't!

ROOTE. *(Shaking him.)* That's my Christmas cake! You can't spit out my Christmas cake!

LUSH. *(Violently, breaking away.)* Stuff it! *(Roote regards him.)*

ROOTE. *(Gravely.)* You've insulted me, you've insulted the cook, and you've insulted Jesus Christ. *(Pause.)* We've got no room for unhealthy minds in this establishment.

LUSH. *(Muttering.)* Muck and slush.

ROOTE. Lush!

LUSH. Colonel?

ROOTE. I said you'd better watch your step. Everyone had better watch their step! *(He begins to move about the room.)* I don't like the look of things. You can't trust a soul And there's something going on here that I haven't quite cottoned on to. There's something funny afoot. I can feel it. Some people think I'm old, but oh no, not by a long chalk. I've got second sight. I can see through walls. *(He considers.)* I don't mean that that's second sight, seeing through walls. I mean I've got second sight *and* I can see through walls!

LUSH. And your knowledge of phytotomy, sir.

ROOTE. That's more than a passing acquaintance. I can see right through them. I can hear a whisper in the basement. I didn't waste my youth. I exercised my faculties — to the hilt! And I spent a lot of time pondering. Pondering. For instance, this stupid business of the world going round. It's all a lot of balls. If the world was going round we'd be falling about all over the room. *(Bending over Lush.)* But are we? Are we? *(Lush considers.)* And today I feel something in my bones. I know it. Something's going on which I can't define. It's ridiculous. But I don't damn well know what it is. Do you think I'm going to be murdered?

LUSH. That's it. *(Roote brings the bottle to the desk and pours.)*

ROOTE. The day got off to a lousy start! A death and a birth. Absolutely bloody scandalous! Is it too much to ask — to keep the place clean? *(Lush goes to the desk, pours a drink, goes back to the armchair.)* You know who you remind me of? You remind me of Whipper Wallace, back in the good old days. *(The door opens. Gibbs enters and stands still.)* He used to hang about with a chap called House-Peters. Boghouse-Peters we used to call him. I remember one day the Whipper and Boghouse — he had a scar on his left cheek, Boghouse — caught in some boghouse brawl, I suppose. *(He laughs.)* Well, anyway, there they were, the Whipper and Boghouse, rolling down the banks of the Euphrates this night, when up came a police-man … *(He dissolves in laughter.)* up came this policeman … up came a policeman … this policeman … approached … Boghouse … and the Whipper … were questioned … this night … the Euphrates … a policeman … *(Gibbs moves. Roote jumps.)* Aaaaahhhh! *(To him.)* What the bloody hell do you think you're doing, creeping up behind me like a snake! Eh? You frightened the life out of me.

GIBBS. I've come to hear the Christmas speech, sir.

ROOTE. Well, why don't you make it? You're dying to make it, aren't you? Why don't you make it?

GIBBS. It's your privilege, sir.

ROOTE. Well, I'm sick to death of it! The patients, the staff, the understaff, the whole damn thing!

GIBBS. I'm sorry to hear that, sir.

ROOTE. It's bleeding me to death.

LUSH. Then why do you continue? *(Roote looks at him.)*

ROOTE. Because I'm a delegate.

LUSH. A delegate of what?

ROOTE. *(Calmly.)* I tell you I'm a delegate.

LUSH. A delegate of what? *(They stare at each other.)*

ROOTE. Not only me. All of us. That bastard there. *(To Gibbs.)* Aren't you?

GIBBS. I am.

ROOTE. There you are.

LUSH. You haven't explained yourself.

ROOTE. Who hasn't?

LUSH. You can't explain yourself.

ROOTE. I can't?

LUSH. Explain yourself.

GIBBS. He's drunk.

ROOTE. *(Moving to him.)* Explain yourself, Lush.

LUSH. No, you! You explain yourself!

ROOTE. Be careful, sonny.

LUSH. *(Rising.)* You're a delegate, are you?

ROOTE. *(Facing him squarely.)* I am.

LUSH. On whose authority? With what power are you entrusted? By whom were you appointed? Of *what* are you a delegate? *(Roote hits him in the stomach.)*

ROOTE. I'm a delegate! *(He hits him in the stomach.)* I was entrusted! *(He hits him in the stomach.)* I'm a delegate! *(He hits him in the stomach.)* I was appointed! *(Lush backs, crouched, slowly across the stage, Roote following him.)* Delegated! *(He hits him in the stomach.)* Appointed! *(He hits him in the stomach.)* Entrusted! *(He hits him in the stomach. Lush sinks to the floor. Roote stands over him and shouts:)* I AM AUTHORISED! *(Lush remains heaped on the floor. Roote goes back to the desk, pours a drink for himself and Gibbs. To Gibbs, sourly.)* What do you want?

GIBBS. I came to hear your Christmas speech, Colonel.

ROOTE. You're sure you didn't come here to murder me?

GIBBS. Murder you?

ROOTE. Yes, wasn't that why you came?

GIBBS. Certainly not. What an idea.

ROOTE. Yes, you did! I can see it in your eyes! Can you see it, Lush, in his eyes? This chap came here to do me in. You can see it in his eyes.

GIBBS. I did no such thing.

ROOTE. You went cross-eyed, man, don't argue with me. Guilty! It was written all over your face.

GIBBS. This is ridiculous.

ROOTE. Yes, well, you're not much good at it, are you? You're pretty poor at it. I twigged it like that! *(He clicks his fingers, laughs.)* Didn't I? You won't get very far as a murderer, will he, Lush? *(Lush begins to stand, slowly.)* Will you?

GIBBS. I resent this levity, sir.

ROOTE. Do you?

GIBBS. I resent it very strongly.

ROOTE. He resents it. *(Going behind the desk with his drink.)* Well, if he resents it he resents it. *(Drinks.)* You're just too sensitive, that's your trouble.

GIBBS. *(Sitting.)* A foul insinuation.

ROOTE. Oh, don't be so touchy! *(Lush walks carefully to Gibbs.)*

LUSH. He was only having a little joke, Gibbs old man.

ROOTE. Of course I was.

GIBBS. I found it less than funny.

LUSH. He didn't mean it. Honestly. Don't be downhearted. Now give me the knife and we won't say another word. *(Sudden silence. All still. Gibbs and Lush stare at each other. Lush makes a tiny movement to his jacket. Immediately Gibbs rises, with a knife in his hand. Lush faces him, a knife in his hand. Roote seizes the bayonet from his desk, comes above them, covering them both, grinning. Silence. All knives up. Suddenly a long sigh is heard, amplified. The knives go down. A long keen is heard, amplified. They look up. A laugh is heard, amplified, dying away. Silence.)* What was that?

ROOTE. I don't know. What was it?

GIBBS. I don't know. *(Pause.)*

ROOTE. I heard something, didn't you?

LUSH. Yes, I did.

GIBBS. Yes, I heard something. *(Pause.)*

ROOTE. Well, what was it? *(Pause.)*

GIBBS. I don't know.

LUSH. Nor do I. *(Pause.)*

ROOTE. Well, is there any way of finding out?

GIBBS. Something's happening, sir. I don't like it. There's something going on … which I can't quite define.

ROOTE. How odd you should say that. I was only saying the same before, wasn't I, Lush? I was saying the same before. Just before you came in. *(Pause.)*

GIBBS. We'll investigate. Come on, Lush.

LUSH. Go yourself.

ROOTE. Go with him.

LUSH. I don't want to go with him.

ROOTE. Go with him! What's the matter? Are you frightened of the dark?

LUSH. *(Shyly.)* No … well, you see, the fact is, Colonel, I've … I've got a present for you.

ROOTE. A present?

LUSH. A Christmas present.

ROOTE. *(Suspiciously.)* Oh yes? What sort of a present?

LUSH. Just a little something, sir, for Christmas. *(He takes a cigar from his pocket and hands it to Roote.)* This is it.

ROOTE. I say! That looks a fine one.

LUSH. Just a little token, sir.

ROOTE. Well, that's a very nice thought, Lush my lad. I'm deeply gratified.

LUSH. I'm glad you like it, sir.

ROOTE. *(Beaming.)* Yes, very nice. I shall smoke it before I go to bed. Now off you go, about your business.

GIBBS. When would you like to see Lamb, sir?

ROOTE. Lamb?

GIBBS. The father, sir.

ROOTE. Oh, him. In the morning, son, in the morning. I can't be bothered to bother with him now. Can I?

GIBBS. In the morning then. Thank you for the drink, sir.

LUSH. And the cake.

ROOTE. Goodnight, gentlemen. *(Gibbs and Lush go out. Roote walks, with the cigar, to the sofa. Miss Cutts appears behind him from the bedroom door, watches him. She wears a nightdress. Roote lights the cigar, puffs. The cigar explodes. Miss Cutts rushes to him. Roote throws the cigar down, sees Miss Cutts.)*

CUTTS. Are you all right? *(Roote stares at her.)* What's the matter with that cigar?

ROOTE. You remind me of someone.

CUTTS. In my new nightie? Who?

ROOTE. Where did you get that thing?

CUTTS. It's a gift. Who do I remind you of?

ROOTE. Where did you get it?

CUTTS. From a friend. Do you like it? She just gave it to me. I had tea with her today. She's a nursing mother. She doesn't need it. She insisted I should have it. She's so sweet, and she's got such a bonny baby. I said to her, now we're friends, I can't go on calling you 6459, can I? What's your name? Do you know, she wouldn't tell me? Well, what does your lover call you? I said, what little nickname? She blushed to the roots of her hair. I must say I'm very curious. What could he have called her? She's sweet, but she said the baby misses his Daddy. Babies do miss Daddy, you know. Archie, can't the baby see his Daddy, just for a little while, just to say hello?

ROOTE. *(Quietly.)* No. Daddy will stay where he is.

CUTTS. Where is he?

ROOTE. You're supposed to be on nightshift.

CUTTS. Oh, it's Christmas, I knocked off early.

ROOTE. You're supposed to be working.

CUTTS. You're not pleased to see me. *(Pause. Roote sighs, looks at her.)*

ROOTE. Are you … *(He sits on the sofa with her.)* Are you … happy?

CUTTS. Happy? Of course I am.

ROOTE. Are you … are you happy with me?

CUTTS. Of course I'm happy. With you. When you're not silly.

ROOTE. You're really happy with me?

CUTTS. Not when you want me to go out into the cold with my nightie on.

ROOTE. *(Taking her hand.)* Don't go out. *(He caresses her hand. She regards him gravely.)*

CUTTS. You know, sometimes I think I'm not feminine enough for you.

ROOTE. You are, you are feminine enough for me.

CUTTS. Perhaps if I was more feminine you wouldn't want me to go out in the cold.

ROOTE. I don't want you to go out. I want you to stay.

CUTTS. Or perhaps … perhaps it's because you think you're not masculine enough.

ROOTE. I am!

CUTTS. Perhaps you're not.

53

ROOTE. You can't want me to be *more* masculine?

CUTTS. *(Urgently.)* It's not what *I* want. It's what *you* really *think*. It's what you really *deeply* think and feel. It's what *you* want, it's what you truly *are*, can't you see that, Archie? I mean, if you're suddenly worried that you're not masculine enough — I mean, that I'm not feminine enough and that you're too feminine — well, it's not going to work, is it?

ROOTE. Now, wait a minute, I never said anything —

CUTTS. *(Intensely.)* If I didn't love you so much it wouldn't matter. Do you remember the first time we met? On the beach? In the night? All those people? And the bonfire? And the waves? And the spray? And the mist? And the moon? Everyone dancing, somersaulting, laughing? And you — standing silent, staring at a sandcastle in your sheer white trunks. The moon was behind you, in front of you, all over you, suffusing you, consuming you, you were transparent, translucent, a beacon. I was struck dumb, dumbstruck. Water rose up my legs. I could not move. I was rigid. Immovable. Our eyes met. Love at first sight. I held your gaze. And in your eyes, bold and unashamed, was desire. Brutal, demanding desire. Bestial, ruthless, remorseless. I stood there magnetised, hypnotised. Transfixed. Motionless and still. A spider caught in a web. *(Roote stands, goes to the desk, sits, switches on the microphone.)*

ROOTE. *(Into the mike.)* Patients, staff and understaff. A merry Christmas to you all, and a happy and prosperous new year. And on behalf of all the staff I'd like to wish all the understaff the very best of luck for the year to come and a very happy Christmas. And to the patients I should like to send a personal greeting, to each and every one of them, wishing them the heartiest compliments of the season, and very best wishes, on behalf of the staff, the understaff and myself, not forgetting the Ministry, which I know would be glad to be associated with these words, for a healthy, happy and prosperous new year. *(Pause.)* We have had our little difficulties, in the year that is about to die, our little troubles, our little sorrows as well as our little joys, but through working together, through each and every one of us pulling his weight, no matter how lowly or apparently trivial his job, by working, by living, by pulling together as one great family, we stand undaunted. *(Pause.)* We say goodbye to the old year very soon now, and hail the new, but I say to you, as we stand before these embers, that we carry with us from the old year ... things ... which will stand us in good stead in the new, and we are not daunted. *(Pause.)* Some of you, sitting at your loudspeakers tonight, may sometimes find yourselves wondering whether the little daily hardships, the little daily disappointments, the trials and tribulations which seem continually to dog you are, in the end, worth it. To you I would say one simple thing. Have faith. *(Pause.)* Yes, I think if I were asked to convey to you a special message this Christmas it would be that: Have faith. *(Pause.)* Remember that you are not alone, that we are here, for example, in this our home, are inextricably related, one to another, the staff to the understaff, the understaff to the patients, the patients to the staff. Remember this, as you sit by your fires, with your families, who have come from near and from far, to share this day with you, and may you be content. *(He switches off the microphone and sits. The lights go down on the office. Darkness. A low light on the stairway and the forestage. Squeaks are heard, of locks turning. The rattle of chains. A great clanging, reverberating, as of iron doors opening. Shafts of light appear abruptly about the stage, as of doors opening into corridors and into rooms. Whispers, chuckles, half-screams of the patients grow. The clanging of locks and doors grows in intensity. The lights shift from area to area, rapidly. The sounds reach a feverish pitch and stop. Lights up on the office in the ministry. Lobb rises as Gibbs enters.)*

LOBB. Ah, come in, Gibbs. How are you? *(They shake hands.)* Have a good journey down?

GIBBS. Not at all bad, thank you, sir.

LOBB. Sit down. *(They sit.)* Cigarette?

GIBBS. No thank you, sir.

LOBB. You haven't been waiting long, have you?

GIBBS. Oh, no sir, not at all.

LOBB. My secretary's down with flu. Rather disorganised. What's the weather like up there?

GIBBS. Quite sharp, sir.

LOBB. Been fair to middling down here, for the time of year. Treacherous, though. My secretary, for instance, quite a stalwart sort of chap, strong as an ox, went down like a log over the weekend.

GIBBS. It's certainly treacherous.

LOBB. Dreadful. How are you feeling yourself?

GIBBS. Oh, I'm quite fit, thank you, sir.

LOBB. Yes, you look fit. Remarkably fit, really. You wear a vest, don't you?

GIBBS. Yes, sir.

LOBB. There you are. Very sensible. My secretary, for instance, strong as an ox, but he never wore a vest in his life. That's what did it. *(Pause.)* Well, I'm glad you got down to see me, Gibbs.

GIBBS. So am I, sir.

LOBB. Rather unfortunate business. You've made out your report, I take it?

GIBBS. Yes, sir.

LOBB. I haven't seen it yet.

GIBBS. No, sir. I have it with me.

LOBB. Hand it in to the office on the way out, will you?

GIBBS. Yes, sir.

LOBB. Got any definite figures?

GIBBS. Yes, I ... have, sir.

LOBB. What are they? *(Pause.)*

GIBBS. The whole staff was slaughtered, sir.

LOBB. The whole staff?

GIBBS. With one exception, of course.

LOBB. Who was that?

GIBBS. Me, sir.

LOBB. Oh yes, of course. *(Pause.)* The whole staff, eh? A massacre, in fact?

GIBBS. Exactly.

LOBB. Most distressing. *(Pause.)* How did they ... how did they do it?

GIBBS. Various means, sir. Mr. Roote and Miss Cutts were stabbed in their bed. Lush —

LOBB. Excuse me, did you say bed, or beds?

GIBBS. Bed, sir.

LOBB. Oh, really? Yes, go on.

GIBBS. Lush, Hogg, Beck, Budd, Tuck, Dodds, Tate and Pett, sir, were hanged and strangled, variously.

LOBB. I see. Well, I should think there's going to be quite a few questions asked about this, Gibbs.

GIBBS. Yes, sir.

LOBB. What's the position now?

GIBBS. The patients are all back in their rooms. I've left the head porter, Tubb, in charge of things. He's very capable. All the understaff, of course, are still active.

LOBB. They didn't touch the understaff?

GIBBS. No. Just the staff.

LOBB. Ah. Look here, Gibbs, there's something I'd like to know. How did the patients get out?

GIBBS. I'm not sure that I can give an absolutely conclusive answer to that, sir, until the proper inquiry has been set in motion.

LOBB. Naturally, naturally.

GIBBS. One possibility though is that one of their doors may not have been properly locked, that the patient got out, filched the keys from the office, and let the others out.

LOBB. Good Lord.

GIBBS. You see, the locktester who should have been on duty — we always had a locktester on duty —

LOBB. Of course, of course.

GIBBS. Was absent from duty.

LOBB. Absent? I say, well ... that's rather ... significant, isn't it?

GIBBS. Yes, sir.

LOBB. What happened to him?

GIBBS. He's ... not to be found, sir.

LOBB. Well, it would be a good thing if he were found, wouldn't it?

GIBBS. I shall do my best, sir.

LOBB. Good-o. *(Slight pause.)* Tell me. Why weren't you killed? Just as a matter of interest?

GIBBS. I was engaged on some research, sir, alone. I was probably the only member of the staff awake, so was able to take measures to protect myself.

LOBB. I see. Well, it's all most unfortunate, but we can't really do anything until the report has gone in and the inquiry set up. Meanwhile you'd better try to get hold of that locktester of yours. I think we shall probably want to have a word with him. What's his name?

GIBBS. Lamb, sir.

LOBB. *(Making a note of the name.)* Lamb. Well, Gibbs, I would like to say on behalf of the Ministry how very much we commend the guts you've shown.

GIBBS. Thank you, sir. My work means a great deal to me.

LOBB. That's the spirit. *(Slight pause.)* You can carry on now, I suppose? We'll have some reinforcements down in a few days. Can't be sooner, I'm afraid. We've got to get hold of some properly qualified people. Not as easy as all that.

GIBBS. I can carry on, sir.

LOBB. You'll be in charge, of course.

GIBBS. Thank you, sir.

LOBB. *(Rising.)* Don't thank me. It's we have to thank you. *(They walk to the door.)* One last question. Why do you think they did it? I mean ... why did they feel so strongly?

GIBBS. Well, Mr. Lobb, it's a little delicate in my position ...

LOBB. Go on, my boy, go on. It's the facts that count.

GIBBS. One doesn't like to speak ill of the dead.

LOBB. Naturally, naturally.

GIBBS. But there's no doubt that Mr. Roote was unpopular.

LOBB. With good cause?

GIBBS. I'm afraid so, sir. Two things especially had made him rather unpopular. He had seduced patient 6459 and been the cause of her pregnancy, and he had murdered patient 6457. That had not gone down too well with the rest of the patients. *(Blackout on office. Lights rise on sound-proof room. Lamb in chair. He sits still, staring as in a catatonic trance.)*

Curtain.

PROPERTY LIST

Office area
> Arm chair
> Desk & chair
> Diary, on desk
> Sofa
> Filing cabinets
> Papers, on desk
> Pencils, on desk
> Drinks cabinet, with bottles & glasses
> Radiator
> Intercom, on desk
> Bayonet, in desk drawer

Sitting Room area
> Coffee machine
> Coffee cups
> Pack of cards
> Internal telephone

Sound-proof Room area
> Electric shock machine, with earphones & red light

Off stage
> Small box, containing cake with microphone in it

Personal
> Eyeglasses, in pocket (Roote)
> Watch (Gibbs)
> Electrodes (2) (Miss Cutts)
> Ping pong ball (Miss Cutts)
> Packet of pills (Gibbs)
> Knife (Gibbs)
> Exploding cigar (Lush)

NEW PLAYS

★ MOTHERHOOD OUT LOUD by Leslie Ayvazian, Brooke Berman, David Cale, Jessica Goldberg, Beth Henley, Lameece Issaq, Claire LaZebnik, Lisa Loomer, Michele Lowe, Marco Pennette, Theresa Rebeck, Luanne Rice, Annie Weisman and Cheryl L. West, conceived by Susan R. Rose and Joan Stein. When entrusting the subject of motherhood to such a dazzling collection of celebrated American writers, what results is a joyous, moving, hilarious, and altogether thrilling theatrical event. "Never fails to strike both the funny bone and the heart." –*BackStage.* "Packed with wisdom, laughter, and plenty of wry surprises." –*TheaterMania.* [1M, 3W] ISBN: 978-0-8222-2589-8

★ COCK by Mike Bartlett. When John takes a break from his boyfriend, he accidentally meets the girl of his dreams. Filled with guilt and indecision, he decides there is only one way to straighten this out. "[A] brilliant and blackly hilarious feat of provocation." –*Independent.* "A smart, prickly and rewarding view of sexual and emotional confusion." –*Evening Standard.* [3M, 1W] ISBN: 978-0-8222-2766-3

★ F. Scott Fitzgerald's THE GREAT GATSBY adapted for the stage by Simon Levy. Jay Gatsby, a self-made millionaire, passionately pursues the elusive Daisy Buchanan. Nick Carraway, a young newcomer to Long Island, is drawn into their world of obsession, greed and danger. "Levy's combination of narration, dialogue and action delivers most of what is best in the novel." –*Seattle Post-Intelligencer.* "A beautifully crafted interpretation of the 1925 novel which defined the Jazz Age." –*London Free Press.* [5M, 4W] ISBN: 978-0-8222-2727-4

★ LONELY, I'M NOT by Paul Weitz. At an age when most people are discovering what they want to do with their lives, Porter has been married and divorced, earned seven figures as a corporate "ninja," and had a nervous breakdown. It's been four years since he's had a job or a date, and he's decided to give life another shot. "Critic's pick!" –*NY Times.* "An enjoyable ride." –*NY Daily News.* [3M, 3W] ISBN: 978-0-8222-2734-2

★ ASUNCION by Jesse Eisenberg. Edgar and Vinny are not racist. In fact, Edgar maintains a blog condemning American imperialism, and Vinny is three-quarters into a Ph.D. in Black Studies. When Asuncion becomes their new roommate, the boys have a perfect opportunity to demonstrate how open-minded they truly are. "Mr. Eisenberg writes lively dialogue that strikes plenty of comic sparks." –*NY Times.* "An almost ridiculously enjoyable portrait of slacker trauma among would-be intellectuals." –*Newsday.* [2M, 2W] ISBN: 978-0-8222-2630-7

DRAMATISTS PLAY SERVICE, INC.
440 Park Avenue South, New York, NY 10016 212-683-8960 Fax 212-213-1539
postmaster@dramatists.com www.dramatists.com

NEW PLAYS

★ **THE PICTURE OF DORIAN GRAY by Roberto Aguirre-Sacasa, based on the novel by Oscar Wilde.** Preternaturally handsome Dorian Gray has his portrait painted by his college classmate Basil Hallwood. When their mutual friend Henry Wotton offers to include it in a show, Dorian makes a fateful wish—that his portrait should grow old instead of him—and strikes an unspeakable bargain with the devil. [5M, 2W] ISBN: 978-0-8222-2590-4

★ **THE LYONS by Nicky Silver.** As Ben Lyons lies dying, it becomes clear that he and his wife have been at war for many years, and his impending demise has brought no relief. When they're joined by their children all efforts at a sentimental goodbye to the dying patriarch are soon abandoned. "Hilariously frank, clear-sighted, compassionate and forgiving." *–NY Times.* "Mordant, dark and rich." *–Associated Press.* [3M, 3W] ISBN: 978-0-8222-2659-8

★ **STANDING ON CEREMONY by Mo Gaffney, Jordan Harrison, Moisés Kaufman, Neil LaBute, Wendy MacLeod, José Rivera, Paul Rudnick, and Doug Wright, conceived by Brian Shnipper.** Witty, warm and occasionally wacky, these plays are vows to the blessings of equality, the universal challenges of relationships, and the often hilarious power of love. "CEREMONY puts a human face on a hot-button issue and delivers laughter and tears rather than propaganda." *–BackStage.* [3M, 3W] ISBN: 978-0-8222-2654-3

★ **ONE ARM by Moisés Kaufman, based on the short story and screenplay by Tennessee Williams.** Ollie joins the Navy and becomes the lightweight boxing champion of the Pacific Fleet. Soon after, he loses his arm in a car accident, and he turns to hustling to survive. "[A] fast, fierce, brutally beautiful stage adaptation." *–NY Magazine.* "A fascinatingly lurid, provocative and fatalistic piece of theater." *–Variety.* [7M, 1W] ISBN: 978-0-8222-2564-5

★ **AN ILIAD by Lisa Peterson and Denis O'Hare.** A modern-day retelling of Homer's classic. Poetry and humor, the ancient tale of the Trojan War and the modern world collide in this captivating theatrical experience. "Shocking, glorious, primal and deeply satisfying." *–Time Out NY.* "Explosive, altogether breathtaking." *–Chicago Sun-Times.* [1M] ISBN: 978-0-8222-2687-1

★ **THE COLUMNIST by David Auburn.** At the height of the Cold War, Joe Alsop is the nation's most influential journalist, beloved, feared and courted by the Washington world. But as the '60s dawn and America undergoes dizzying change, the intense political dramas Joe is embroiled in become deeply personal as well. "Intensely satisfying." *–Bloomberg News.* [5M, 2W] ISBN: 978-0-8222-2699-4

DRAMATISTS PLAY SERVICE, INC.
440 Park Avenue South, New York, NY 10016 212-683-8960 Fax 212-213-1539
postmaster@dramatists.com www.dramatists.com

NEW PLAYS

★ **BENGAL TIGER AT THE BAGHDAD ZOO by Rajiv Joseph.** The lives of two American Marines and an Iraqi translator are forever changed by an encounter with a quick-witted tiger who haunts the streets of war-torn Baghdad. "[A] boldly imagined, harrowing and surprisingly funny drama." *–NY Times.* "Tragic yet darkly comic and highly imaginative." *–CurtainUp.* [5M, 2W] ISBN: 978-0-8222-2565-2

★ **THE PITMEN PAINTERS by Lee Hall, inspired by a book by William Feaver.** Based on the triumphant true story, a group of British miners discover a new way to express themselves and unexpectedly become art-world sensations. "Excitingly ambiguous, in-the-moment theater." *–NY Times.* "Heartfelt, moving and deeply politicized." *–Chicago Tribune.* [5M, 2W] ISBN: 978-0-8222-2507-2

★ **RELATIVELY SPEAKING by Ethan Coen, Elaine May and Woody Allen.** In TALKING CURE, Ethan Coen uncovers the sort of insanity that can only come from family. Elaine May explores the hilarity of passing in GEORGE IS DEAD. In HONEYMOON MOTEL, Woody Allen invites you to the sort of wedding day you won't forget. "Firecracker funny." *–NY Times.* "A rollicking good time." *–New Yorker.* [8M, 7W] ISBN: 978-0-8222-2394-8

★ **SONS OF THE PROPHET by Stephen Karam.** If to live is to suffer, then Joseph Douaihy is more alive than most. With unexplained chronic pain and the fate of his reeling family on his shoulders, Joseph's health, sanity, and insurance premium are on the line. "Explosively funny." *–NY Times.* "At once deep, deft and beautifully made." *–New Yorker.* [5M, 3W] ISBN: 978-0-8222-2597-3

★ **THE MOUNTAINTOP by Katori Hall.** A gripping reimagination of events the night before the assassination of the civil rights leader Dr. Martin Luther King, Jr. "An ominous electricity crackles through the opening moments." *–NY Times.* "[A] thrilling, wild, provocative flight of magical realism." *–Associated Press.* "Crackles with theatricality and a humanity more moving than sainthood." *–NY Newsday.* [1M, 1W] ISBN: 978-0-8222-2603-1

★ **ALL NEW PEOPLE by Zach Braff.** Charlie is 35, heartbroken, and just wants some time away from the rest of the world. Long Beach Island seems to be the perfect escape until his solitude is interrupted by a motley parade of misfits who show up and change his plans. "Consistently and sometimes sensationally funny." *–NY Times.* "A morbidly funny play about the trendy new existential condition of being young, adorable, and miserable." *–Variety.* [2M, 2W] ISBN: 978-0-8222-2562-1

DRAMATISTS PLAY SERVICE, INC.
440 Park Avenue South, New York, NY 10016 212-683-8960 Fax 212-213-1539
postmaster@dramatists.com www.dramatists.com

NEW PLAYS

★ **CLYBOURNE PARK by Bruce Norris.** WINNER OF THE 2011 PULITZER PRIZE AND 2012 TONY AWARD. Act One takes place in 1959 as community leaders try to stop the sale of a home to a black family. Act Two is set in the same house in the present day as the now predominantly African-American neighborhood battles to hold its ground. "Vital, sharp-witted and ferociously smart." –*NY Times*. "A theatrical treasure…Indisputably, uproariously funny." –*Entertainment Weekly*. [4M, 3W] ISBN: 978-0-8222-2697-0

★ **WATER BY THE SPOONFUL by Quiara Alegría Hudes.** WINNER OF THE 2012 PULITZER PRIZE. A Puerto Rican veteran is surrounded by the North Philadelphia demons he tried to escape in the service. "This is a very funny, warm, and yes uplifting play." –*Hartford Courant*. "The play is a combination poem, prayer and app on how to cope in an age of uncertainty, speed and chaos." –*Variety*. [4M, 3W] ISBN: 978-0-8222-2716-8

★ **RED by John Logan.** WINNER OF THE 2010 TONY AWARD. Mark Rothko has just landed the biggest commission in the history of modern art. But when his young assistant, Ken, gains the confidence to challenge him, Rothko faces the agonizing possibility that his crowning achievement could also become his undoing. "Intense and exciting." –*NY Times*. "Smart, eloquent entertainment." –*New Yorker*. [2M] ISBN: 978-0-8222-2483-9

★ **VENUS IN FUR by David Ives.** Thomas, a beleaguered playwright/director, is desperate to find an actress to play Vanda, the female lead in his adaptation of the classic sadomasochistic tale *Venus in Fur*. "Ninety minutes of good, kinky fun." –*NY Times*. "A fast-paced journey into one man's entrapment by a clever, vengeful female." –*Associated Press*. [1M, 1W] ISBN: 978-0-8222-2603-1

★ **OTHER DESERT CITIES by Jon Robin Baitz.** Brooke returns home to Palm Springs after a six-year absence and announces that she is about to publish a memoir dredging up a pivotal and tragic event in the family's history—a wound they don't want reopened. "Leaves you feeling both moved and gratifyingly sated." –*NY Times*. "A genuine pleasure." –*NY Post*. [2M, 3W] ISBN: 978-0-8222-2605-5

★ **TRIBES by Nina Raine.** Billy was born deaf into a hearing family and adapts brilliantly to his family's unconventional ways, but it's not until he meets Sylvia, a young woman on the brink of deafness, that he finally understands what it means to be understood. "A smart, lively play." –*NY Times*. "[A] bright and boldly provocative drama." –*Associated Press*. [3M, 2W] ISBN: 978-0-8222-2751-9

DRAMATISTS PLAY SERVICE, INC.
440 Park Avenue South, New York, NY 10016 212-683-8960 Fax 212-213-1539
postmaster@dramatists.com www.dramatists.com